SPECIAL DIET COOKBOOKS
GLUTEN-FREE COOKING

Practical and delicious recipes for every occasion —
catering imaginatively for those who need to have
gluten excluded from their diet.

SPECIAL DIET COOKBOOKS
GLUTEN-FREE COOKING

Rita Greer

Illustrations by the author

Thorsons
An Imprint of HarperCollins*Publishers*

Thorsons
An Imprint of HarperCollins*Publishers*
77–85 Fulham Palace Road,
Hammersmith, London W6 8JB

First published 1978
Second edition, revised,
enlarged and reset, 1983
Third edition 1989
7 9 10 8 6

A catalogue record for this book
is available from the British Library

ISBN 0 7225 2201 0

Printed and bound in Great Britain by
Mackays of Chatham PLC, Chatham, Kent

CONTENTS

1.

COOKING FOR A GLUTEN-FREE DIET

The sudden introduction of a special diet into the running of a household can be a traumatic experience. Often there is very little help available at the crucial beginning of the diet, especially if there is no dietitian to give advice. If the situation is badly handled the special dieter can quite unintentionally be made to feel abnormal and a nuisance. A child on a strict diet can instinctively feel he or she is a source of worry as the mealtime routine is suddenly changed.

My advice is don't get into a panic and don't despair. Instead, direct your energy into getting reorganized in the kitchen in order to cope with the new and challenging situation on your domestic front. Hundreds of thousands of people all over the world are in your predicament, so don't feel you are alone and that the problem is gigantic. It isn't anything that cannot be sorted out easily.

SOME QUESTIONS ANSWERED

What exactly is gluten?

If you take a spoonful of wheat flour and mix it with a little water the result will be an elastic sort of paste, firmly bound together. The ingredient that makes it bind like this is the *gluten* in the wheat — the 'elastic'. The gluten is actually protein and in a normal diet is a valuable addition. A similar effect is obtained when mixing rye, barley or oat flour with water. Items such as bread can have extra gluten added, as in the so-called 'strong' flours. However, it does not hurt anyone to live without it and millions of people all over the world go the whole of their lives without ever having eaten it, with no ill effects.

Where is gluten found?

It is found mainly in wheat, but also in rye, barley and oats. It is only found in *grains* and the diagram below shows what they look like before they are ground into flour. *Note:* There is no gluten in rice although it is an important grain product.

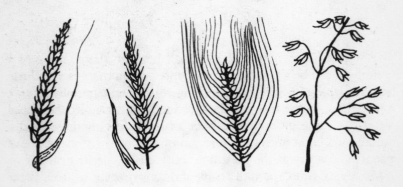

What are wheat, rye, barley and oats used for?

These are mainly used for making bread, cakes, biscuits, pastry and breakfast cereals. Wheat is the most widely used of the four. They are also added to products to thicken them and make them smooth and to help bind them together. For example they can be put into the sauce that goes with baked beans and into instant puddings.

The flour you buy in the shops for baking is wheat flour, whether plain or self-raising, and the same flour is used in commercial baking for shop bread, cakes, pastries, buns, biscuits etc.

Are any gluten-free items readily available?

Yes, lots! All fruit and vegetables, meat, fish, pulses, eggs, cheese, milk, butter, margarine, cooking oils and nuts are gluten-free.

Is gluten-free cooking more difficult than ordinary cooking?

Old fashioned gluten-free cooking was difficult and dull, but the new recipes in this book will show you that in most cases it is easier and more delicious than ordinary cooking.

How can you tell which commercial products contain gluten?

Look carefully at the labels of the products. There should be a special 'box' which lists the ingredients. The following may indicate the presence of gluten:

Bran	Oats
Wheatgerm	Oatmeal
Wheat bran	Rolled Oats
Wholewheat	Oat flour
Wholegrain	Edible starch
Wheatmeal	Food starch
Wheat flour	Special gluten-free food starch
Wheat starch	(usually wheat starch in
Wheat protein	disguise)
Rye	Rusk
Rye flour	Flour
Barley	Starch
Pearl barley	Thickening
Barley meal	Cornflour (cornstarch)

'Starch' can mean anything from wheat flour to potato flour. 'Cornflour' can also cover a multitude of sins and can mean all sorts of starches mixed up (UK).

You will find instructions on how to approach manufacturers for information on page 11.

Here is a list of common products likely to contain gluten. Although it is a long list, don't worry! Most of it is 'junk' food and is best avoided in any case.

Gravy powders
Breakfast cereals
Cocoa
Baby foods
Soups (in packets and tins)
Pastes
Bedtime drinks
Drinking Chocolate
Pasta
Spaghetti
Macaroni
Baked beans
Baking powders
   (raising powders)
Salad dressings
Sandwich spreads
Cakes
Crispbreads
Porridge
Muesli
Cereals (based on
   wheat/oats)

White pepper
Mustard (dry or made up)
Sauces
Chutneys, pickles
Yogurt
Pie fillings
Instant puddings
Blancmange
Custard
Cornflour (cornstarch)
Instant coffee
Curry powder
Sausages
Breadcrumbs
Bread
Biscuits (cookies)
Batter, batter mixes
Crumble topping
Cake mixes
Biscuit/bun mixes
Stock cubes
Cheap chocolate

For a list of gluten-free products see page 122.

Are there any commercial gluten-free flours?
Yes, there are. They are usually made from a grain which contains

gluten — usually wheat — which is processed to take out the gluten, *as far as possible*. What remains is virtually pure starch (wheat starch) and is labelled 'gluten-free'. However, there is no way of extracting *all* the gluten and so it cannot be guaranteed 100 per cent gluten-free. (Probably 'low-gluten' is a better description of such flour.) It has a wide use in low-protein diets and consequently has a low nutritional value as well as being difficult to use and unpalatable. It is cheap and widely available because it is a by-product of the slimming food industry which is always in need of gluten as a protein.

Are there any types of flour which are naturally gluten-free?

Yes, there are five major ones: rice flour, maize flour (cornmeal), potato flour, soya flour and pea flour. All these are used in the recipes in this book.

Is there any way you can find out which products contain gluten?

There are societies specially for people on gluten-free diets who publish lists of gluten-free foods. Unless such societies are enthusiastic, very active, and publish a new list annually, the lists tend to be outdated and therefore misleading. Another danger is that some organizations may have favourite manufacturers and will deliberately ignore products by rival manufacturing companies, thus giving the gluten-free consumer a limited list of products that are available. By being a member of these societies such lists may (but not necessarily) be made available to you.

You can also approach manufacturers for lists. The best way is to write a straightforward letter, enclosing a stamped addressed envelope, requesting a list of their products which are gluten-free. The larger firms have these lists printed off ready for such enquiries but some firms do not reply on principle. Here is a sample letter to a firm.

Dear Sirs,

Gluten-free Products

I am cooking for a gluten-free diet and would be most grateful if you would advise me as to which of your products are gluten-free. I enclose a stamped addressed envelope.

Yours faithfully,

It is a good idea to keep a pocket notebook with your own lists of products to avoid. This will prove very helpful when out shopping.

2.

THE KITCHEN CUPBOARD

Clear out a particular corner or shelf in your kitchen for the special items you are going to need for baking and cooking. Some of the items you can make for yourself and some you can buy. All of them are suitable for the whole family so don't think it is going to be that difficult to organize.

Contamination

One of the problems of gluten-free baking is to avoid contamination by gluten-containing flours such as wheat. It can occur by contact with other items in the kitchen and store cupboard such as wheat flour; by using utensils and equipment which are also used for ordinary cooking, e.g. baking tins; and by airborne means such as flour dust from overalls and aprons. Other dangers are wheat flour under the finger-nails and wheat breadcrumbs in the toaster.

If cooking for an acutely allergic person, separate baking tins and utensils are essential. If cooking for a not-so-allergic person, ordinary tins etc. can be used if they are kept scrupulously clean.

Essentials for the Kitchen Cupboard

Cooking oil (sunflower, soya, corn)

Pure almond and vanilla flavourings

Rice paper

Soya sauce (thin, gluten-free)

Ground brown rice

Maize flour (cornmeal)

Potato flour

Yellow split pea flour

Soya flour

Wine or cider vinegar

Dried yeast

Spices (ginger, nutmeg,
  mixed spice — gluten-free
  brand — allspice, ground
  cloves, cinnamon etc.)

Raw cane sugars

Dried pectin

Black peppercorns

Gelatine crystals

Fruit juices

Trufree or *Jubilee* flours (all
  100 per cent gluten-free)

3.

EMERGENCY GLUTEN-FREE MENUS

Just to give you a practical helping hand to start, here are some emergency menus that can easily be followed until you have found sources of the few special ingredients and products you will need for a new and interesting diet.

Adults

Eat only the foods specified. They are easily obtainable and most will already be in the store cupboard or refrigerator. Use sea salt and freshly ground black pepper for seasoning. Put polyunsaturated margarine or butter on hot vegetables. Drink tea or coffee with milk. Wine, port, sherry and brandies may be drunk, but no other types of alcohol.

Breakfast:
Rice Krispies (UK), milk and raw cane sugar; grilled bacon, poached or fried egg, grilled tomatoes, fried mushrooms; pure fruit juice. Don't be tempted to eat bread or any other breakfast cereals. If *Rice Krispies* are unobtainable, make a muesli-type cereal yourself from 1 to 2 heaped tablespoonsful of cold cooked brown rice (boiled the previous day), a sprinkling each of raisins, sesame and sunflower seeds, an eating apple (grated), a little liquid honey to sweeten and milk or fruit juice to moisten.

Midday meal:
Boiled or baked-in-skin potatoes; fresh salad of tomatoes, lettuce, cucumber, grated carrot; tinned salmon, tuna or sardines in oil or water. Make a dressing from 2 teaspoonsful sunflower oil (or similar),

a squeeze of fresh lemon juice, a pinch or two of raw cane sugar, sea salt and freshly ground black pepper. If you wish to eat a dessert of some kind, choose any type of fresh fruit — bananas, grapes, apples, oranges, pears etc.

Dinner:
Grilled lamb chop or small steak; 2 plain boiled or steamed green vegetables — cabbage, French (snap) beans, peas, sprouts etc.; plain brown rice, boiled. If you feel the need for a gravy, save the meat juices from the grill pan, strain them off, discard the fat and pour in some of the water strained from the vegetables. Mix well with a wooden spoon and add half a ripe tomato, mashed. Season to taste. Do not use any kind of gravy mix.

Snacks:
Allow yourself up to 3 bananas per day, a few plain almonds or walnuts (English walnuts) and dried fruits such as apricots and raisins.

Eating out is a problem and best avoided when you start the diet. At home stick to plain, fresh ingredients and you will have no worries.

Other foods you might like to choose from are:

Cold ham (without breadcrumb coating);
Cold lamb, beef or pork (off a previously roasted joint without stuffing);
Roast beef or lamb with roast potatoes;
Boiled root vegetables such as carrots, parsnips, turnips.

Without bread, cakes and biscuits (cookies) your starch intake will be too low. Eat plenty of potatoes and rice to make up for this.

Bear in mind that these are emergency menus and are a little narrow in outlook for a long-term gluten-free diet. However, with this information you should be able to get started immediately rather than continue with an ordinary diet until you have reorganized your eating regime in a broader way. No matter how tempting, *do not eat bread, cakes and biscuits* etc.

Here is a shopping list/storecupboard check for emergency menus:

Rice Krispies (if available)
Milk
Raw cane sugar
Bacon
Eggs
Pure fruit juice
Sesame and sunflower seeds
Fresh meat
Fresh fruit
Dried fruit
Fresh vegetables
Tomato *Purée* (paste)

Cooking oil (vegetable oil)
Almonds and walnuts (English walnuts)
Sea salt
Black peppercorns
Salmon, tuna (tunny), sardines — all canned in oil or water
Brown rice (plain)
Butter or margarine
Tea or coffee

Emergency Menus for Children

Use the emergency menus for adults but omit the alcohol and add extra snacks such as:

Fresh orange segments sprinkled with a little raw cane sugar;

Home-made fish cakes — (see recipe page 26);

Home-made chips — peel and chip fresh potatoes. Fry in deep, hot oil until golden. Drain on kitchen paper and serve hot with a poached egg on top and grilled tomatoes instead of tomato sauce;

Savoury rice — fry a small chopped onion in a little oil. Add chopped cooked vegetables and 1 cupful (1¼ cupsful) of cold cooked brown rice. Heat through while turning over with a wooden spoon. Season and serve;

Milk shakes — blend 2 cupsful of milk with any piece of stoned, peeled fruit. Add raw cane sugar to taste and blend. (You will need a blender/liquidizer for this.)

4.

STAPLE SUBSTITUTES

There is one very important food around which a gluten-free diet revolves. This is bread, and life without it can be difficult; there is no way to fill the gap left by wheat bread other than to substitute another kind that is just as nutritious and versatile. Here are four recipes for gluten-free bread which are easy to make and comfortably fill this gap. (They are also easier to make than ordinary bread.)

'PLAIN' LOAF

This loaf has an attractive golden crust and a creamy coloured centre. All the ingredients are naturally pale in colour (i.e. they are not bleached or processed to make them pale). The flour blend used comprises naturally gluten-free flours based on wholefood principles. The brown specks in the flour are caused by the brown skins on the wholeground almonds which are part of the blend.

Imperial (Metric)
10¼ oz (290g) *Trufree* No. 4 flour
1 tablespoonful vegetable oil
1 sachet of yeast (provided with the flour)
Exactly 8 fl oz (225ml) warm water

American
2½ cupsful *Trufree* No. 4 flour
1 tablespoonful vegetable oil
1 sachet of yeast (provided with the flour)
1 cupful warm water

1. Preheat oven at 350°F/180°C (Gas Mark 4).

2. Put the flour in a bowl, add the oil and sprinkle in the yeast.

3.   Stir well, pour in the water and mix to a creamy batter.

4.   Spoon into a greased 1 lb (½ kilo) loaf tin and place immediately on the top shelf of the oven to bake.

5.   When golden brown, well risen and crusty (after about an hour), turn out of the tin and cool on a wire rack.

6.   Do not cut until cold. Store in a clean, sealed polythene bag.

Note: This bread does not have to be kneaded or proved (left to rise). It takes only a minute to prepare and can be sliced thinly, toasted or fried. This recipe will only work with *Trufree* No. 4 or No. 5 flours. The size of the tin is important — it should be 6 × 3½ × 2¾ in. (15 × 9 × 7cm).

CRUSTY BROWN BREAD
Make and bake exactly as for Crusty 'Plain' Bread but use *Trufree* No. 5 flour which is brown.

Note: If you cannot obtain *Trufree* flours, the flour blends can be made at home.

CRUSTY 'PLAIN' BREAD

Imperial (Metric)	American
2 slightly heaped teaspoonsful dried yeast granules	2 slightly heaped teaspoonsful dried yeast granules
9 fl oz (250ml) warm water	1 cupful plus 2½ tablespoonsful warm water
1 heaped teaspoonful raw cane sugar	1 heaped tablespoonful raw cane sugar
1 oz (25g) soya flour	¼ cupful soya flour
4½ oz (115g) potato flour (farina)	¾ cupful plus 1 tablespoonful potato flour (farina)
¾ oz (20g) yellow split pea flour	1½ tablespoonsful yellow split pea flour
¾ oz (20g) ground almonds	1½ tablespoonsful ground almonds
2 teaspoonsful dried pectin to bind	2 teaspoonsful dried pectin to bind
2 pinches of sea salt	2 pnches of sea salt
2 teaspoonsful vegetable oil	2 teaspoonsful vegetable oil

1. Preheat the oven at 350°F/180°C (Gas Mark 4).

2. Sprinkle the yeast into the warm water with the sugar. Leave to soften for 3 or 4 minutes.

3. Put all the other ingredients into a bowl and mix well with the hands, breaking up any lumps.

4. Stir the yeast, water and sugar and pour on to the flour mixture.

5. Mix, then beat to a creamy consistency, with a wooden spoon. (Do not use an electric beater as this will make the batter too tough.)

6. Grease a medium-sized loaf tin with oil and flour with maize (cornmeal) or potato flour. (Tin size should be 7¼ × 3½ × 2¼ in. or 185×90×50mm.)

7. Use a wooden spoon to place the mixture in the tin and put straight in the oven on the top shelf.

8. Bake for about 1 hour until well risen, golden and crusty.

9. Turn out on to a wire rack to cool as soon as you take it out of the oven. (Do not cut until cold.)

Note: Use this loaf as ordinary bread. Keep it stored in a clean, sealed polythene bag. This size loaf should last you 2 or 3 days. (If fresh yeast is to be used, allow double the amount.)

BROWN LOAF

Imperial (Metric)
2 slightly heaped teaspoonsful yeast
    granules
9 fl oz (250ml) warm water
1 heaped teaspoonful raw cane
    sugar
1 oz (25g) soya flour
4½ oz (115g) ground brown rice
¾ oz (20g) yellow split pea flour
2 teaspoonsful dried pectin to bind
½ oz (15g) ground almonds
3 pinches of sea salt
3 teaspoonsful vegetable oil
1 heaped teaspoonful carob powder

American
2 slightly heaped teaspoonsful yeast
    granules
1 cupful plus 2½ tablespoonsful
    warm water
1 heaped teaspoonful raw cane
    sugar
¼ cupful soya flour
½ cupful plus 1 tablespoonful ground
    brown rice
1½ tablespoonsful yellow split pea
    flour
2 teaspoonsful dried pectin to bind
1 tablespoonful ground almonds
3 pinches of sea salt
3 teaspoonsful vegetable oil
1 heaped teaspoonful carob powder

1. Preheat the oven at 350°F/180°C (Gas Mark 4).

2. Sprinkle the yeast into the warm water with the sugar, and leave to soften for a few minutes.

3. Put all other ingredients into a bowl and mix well with the hands, breaking up any lumps.

4. Stir the yeast, water and sugar and pour on to the flour mixture.

5. Mix then beat with a wooden spoon. (Do not use an electric beater as this will make the batter too tough.)

6. Grease a medium-sized loaf tin with oil and flour with maize (cornmeal) flour or potato flour. (Tin size should be 7¼ × 3½ × 2¼ in. or 185 × 90 × 50mm.)

Note: This loaf does not rise quite as high as the 'plain' version, but will make a nice crusty loaf with a good texture. Toast, fry etc. as for ordinary bread. (If fresh yeast is to be used, you will need twice the amount as for dried.)

SODA BREAD

This is the poor relation of bread made with yeast. It must be used within a few hours of baking as it does dry out. However, it is sometimes useful to be able to make a quick loaf which will bake in 20 minutes.

Imperial (Metric)	American
½ lb (¼ kilo) *Trufree* No. 4 flour	2 cupsful *Trufree* No. 4 flour
1 teaspoonful raw cane sugar	1 teaspoonful raw cane sugar
1 heaped teaspoonful bicarbonate of soda	1 heaped teaspoonful baking soda
1 heaped teaspoonful cream of tartar	1 heaped teaspoonful cream of tartar
1 tablespoonful vegetable oil	1 tablespoonful vegetable oil
¼ pint (150ml) cold milk	⅔ cupful cold milk

1.   Preheat oven at 425°F/220°C (Gas Mark 7).

2.   Put the flour into a bowl with the sugar, bicarbonate of soda (baking soda) and cream of tartar, and mix really well.

3.   Spoon in the oil and rub in with the fingers.

4.   Pour in the milk and mix to a stiff dough. Knead, using more of the flour, into a round loaf.

5.   Put the loaf on to a greased baking sheet and bake for about 20 minutes, cutting the top with a knife into the traditional cross.

6.   Cool on a wire rack.

Variation: 1 oz (25g)/¼ cupful of dried fruit can be added to the flour to make tea-bread.

CRISPBREADS

Imperial (Metric)	American
½ oz (15g) rice bran	1 tablespoonful rice bran
Pinch of sea salt	Pinch of sea salt
3½ oz (90g) *Trufree* No. 6 plain flour	½ cupful less 1 tablespoonful *Trufree* No. 6 plain flour
1 oz (25g) polyunsaturated soft margarine	2½ tablespoonsful polyunsaturated soft margarine
3 tablespoonsful cold water	3½ tablespoonsful cold water

1. Preheat oven at 450°F/230°C (Gas Mark 8).

2. Put the rice bran into a bowl with the salt and flour. Mix well.

3. Add the margarine and rub it in with the fingers until the mixture resembles fine breadcrumbs.

4. Add the cold water and mix into one lump of dough.

5. Roll out, using more flour, into a thin sheet of dough. Use a knife to cut into about 8 rectangles.

6. Use a spatula to lift them on to ungreased baking sheets and prick all over with a fork.

7. Bake for about 15 minutes and remove from baking sheets with a spatula. Leave to cool and crisp on a wire rack.

8. When cold, store in an air-tight container.

Note: Eat these with cheese and celery as an alternative to bread. Good for picnics.

WATER BISCUITS
(Makes about 12 to 15)

Imperial (Metric)
4 oz (100g) *Trufree* No. 6 plain flour
1 oz (25g) polyunsaturated soft
  margarine
2 pinches of sea salt
Cold water to mix
Extra *Trufree* flour for rolling out etc.

American
½ cupful *Trufree* No. 6 plain flour
2½ tablespoonsful polyunsaturated
  soft margarine
2 pinches of sea salt
Cold water to mix
Extra *Trufree* flour for rolling out etc.

1. Preheat oven at 450°F/230°C (Gas Mark 8).

2. Put the flour into a basin with the margarine and salt and rub in with the fingers until the mixture resembles fine breadcrumbs.

3. Add a little water (to release the binder in the flour) and mix to a stiff paste with a fork. Add more water if required.

4. Knead quickly into one lump of soft dough.

5. Roll out thinly and cut into squares or rectangles.

6. Use a spatula to place them on ungreased baking sheets. Prick with a fork.

7. Bake for about 8 to 10 minutes on the top shelf until golden but not brown.

8. Remove the biscuits from the baking sheets and leave them to cool and crisp up on a wire rack.

9. Store in an air-tight container.

5.

BREAKFASTS

FISH CAKES
(Makes about 6)

These fish cakes can be made in advance, stored in the fridge and fried as required. Do not keep for more than 36 hours before using.

Imperial (Metric)	American
½ lb (¼ kilo) cooked fish such as haddock, cod or coley	1¼ cupsful cooked fish such as haddock, cod or coley
½ lb (¼ kilo) cold, boiled potato	1 cupful cold, boiled potato
1 oz (25g) polyunsaturated soft margarine	2½ tablespoonsful polyunsaturated soft margarine
1 heaped tablespoonful freshly chopped parsley	1 heaped tablespoonful freshly chopped parsley
Sea salt and freshly ground black pepper	Sea salt and freshly ground black pepper
Vegetable oil for frying	Vegetable oil for frying

1. Mash the fish with the potatoes and the margarine.

2. Add the remaining ingredients and mix well with a fork until the fish and parsley are evenly distributed.

3. Form into round, flat cakes with the hands.

4. Fry in hot, shallow oil for 3 minutes on each side or longer if the fish cakes have been in the fridge.

5. Serve immediately with grilled tomatoes and special gluten-free bread and margarine or butter.

Variations: Tinned salmon or tuna (in water or oil) may be used instead of white fish. (Drain well before using.)

As alternatives to just plain frying, try dipping the fish cakes in beaten egg and roll them in special gluten-free breadcrumbs before frying; or brush them with milk and dip them in special gluten-free breadcrumbs.

Note: Commercially-made fish cakes often use wheat-bread crumbs as a coating.

MUESLI

Imperial (Metric)	American
1-2 tablespoonsful of a suitable base — cold cooked brown rice or *Trufree Crispbran*	1-2½ tablespoonsful of a suitable base — cold cooked brown rice or *Trufree Crispbran*
1 ripe eating apple, washed and sliced	1 ripe eating apple, washed and sliced
½ a ripe banana (optional), sliced	½ a ripe banana (optional), sliced
1 tablespoonful raisins	1 tablespoonful raisins
1 tablespoonful chopped nuts	1 tablespoonful chopped nuts
1 teaspoonful sesame seeds	1 teaspoonful sesame seeds
1 teaspoonful sunflower seeds	1 teaspoonful sunflower seeds
Diluted fruit juice or milk	Diluted fruit juice or milk
Raw cane sugar to taste (optional)	Raw cane sugar to taste (optional)

1. Put all the ingredients into a cereal bowl.

2. Pour over the juice or milk and serve.

Note: Other dried fruits can be used such as chopped dried apricots or peaches, stoned prunes etc. If fresh fruit is not available, soaked dried fruit salad can be used for variation. To save time, a basic muesli of dry items can be made, stored in an air-tight jar and used as required. This way more variety can be achieved.

MUESLI BASE

Imperial (Metric)
2 oz (50g) raisins
3 oz (75g) chopped nuts — walnuts, cashews, Brazils etc.
2 oz (50g) sesame seeds
3 oz (75g) sunflower seeds
1 oz (25g) ground almonds
2 oz (50g) chopped dried apricots
2 oz (50g) chopped stoned prunes
4 oz (100g) *Trufree Crispbran*

American
1/3 cupful raisins
2/3 cupful chopped nuts — English walnuts, cashews, Brazils etc.
1/3 cupful sesame seeds
3/4 cupful sunflower seeds
1/4 cupful ground almonds
1/3 cupful chopped dried apricots
1/3 cupful chopped stoned prunes
2/3 cupful *Trufree Crispbran*

1.   Combine all the ingredients.

2.   Store in an air-tight jar and use as required.

Note: Use as a base with fresh fruit, raw cane sugar or liquid honey to taste and milk to moisten.

RICE PORRIDGE
This is good for cold winter mornings. Follow with grilled bacon and special gluten-free bread fried on one side in hot vegetable oil.

Imperial (Metric)
1/2 pint (1/4 litre) milk
2 tablespoonsful ground brown rice
2 teaspoonsful vegetable oil
1 tablespoonful sultanas or chopped dried apricots
2 heaped teaspoonful raw cane sugar
1/2 oz (15g) ground almonds

American
1 1/3 cupsful milk
2 1/2 tablespoonsful ground brown rice
2 teaspoonsful vegetable oil
1 tablespoonful golden seedless raisins or chopped dried apricots
2 heaped teaspoonsful raw cane sugar
2 1/2 tablespoonsful ground almonds

1.   Put the milk and ground rice into a saucepan and stir until smooth.

2.   Add the oil and dried fruit and heat to boiling point. Cook while

stirring with a wooden spoon for a few minutes until the porridge thickens and the fruit swells.

3. Add the sugar and almonds. Stir well and serve hot.

POTATO AND BEANS

Imperial (Metric)
Vegetable oil for frying
2 baked or boiled potatoes, cut into slices
1 portion gluten-free baked beans in tomato sauce

American
Vegetable oil for frying
2 baked or boiled potatoes, cut into slices
1 portion gluten-free baked beans in tomato sauce

1. Put a little oil in the frying pan and heat. Add the potato slices and cook on both sides until golden and crisp.

2. At the same time, heat the beans in a small saucepan.

3. Serve at once on a warmed plate.

Note: The potatoes can be cooked the day before, either baked in their skins or boiled in salted water.

BEANS ON TOAST

Toast thick slices of special gluten-free bread. Spread with polyunsaturated soft margarine and top with hot gluten-free baked beans in tomato sauce.

BUBBLE AND SQUEAK

Fry leftover greens and potato (pre-cooked and chopped up) in the frying pan with a little vegetable oil to prevent it sticking. Turn over and fry on the other side. Season with sea salt and freshly ground black pepper. Serve hot with grilled bacon.

KEDGEREE

Although this sounds a rather strange dish for breakfast, it was a popular item on the menu for the Victorian breakfast table as it made use of the leftovers of the previous day. It could certainly be made the night before and reheated for breakfast.

Imperial (Metric)	American
2-3 heaped tablespoonsful cooked brown rice	2¹/₂-3¹/₂ heaped tablespoonsful cooked brown rice
2 oz (50g) cooked, flaked haddock or cod	¹/₃ cupful cooked, flaked haddock or cod
1 medium-sized tomato, chopped small	1 medium-sized tomato, chopped small
1 egg, hard-boiled	1 egg, hard-boiled
Sea salt and freshly ground black pepper	Sea salt and freshly ground black pepper
Vegetable oil	Vegetable oil

1. Mix together the first three ingredients and season.

2. Heat a little oil in a saucepan. Add the rice mixture and heat through while stirring gently. Top with chopped hard-boiled egg.

3. Season and serve hot on a warmed plate.

BREAKFAST PLATTER

Imperial (Metric)	American
2 oz (50g) lamb's liver	1 small piece lamb's liver
Maize flour	Cornmeal
2 slices back bacon	2 slices back bacon
2 slices special gluten-free bread	2 slices special gluten-free bread
2 medium-sized tomatoes	2 medium-sized tomatoes

1. Wash the liver and cut out any strings etc., then cut it into strips.

2. Dip the strips in maize flour (cornmeal) and fry in a little hot vegetable oil.

3. At the same time, put the bacon, bread and tomatoes under a hot grill, turning the bread over to toast both sides.

4. Serve on a warmed plate with the tomatoes on the toast.

Variation: Fry 3 or 4 sliced mushrooms with the liver.

LEMON PANCAKES
(Makes 3)

Imperial (Metric)
2 oz (50g) *Trufree* No. 7 S.R. flour
1 egg
¼ pint (150ml) milk or milk and
   water
Pinch of sea salt
Vegetable oil for frying
Raw cane sugar
Fresh lemon juice

American
¼ cupful *Trufree* No. 7 S.R. flour
1 egg
⅔ cupful milk or milk and water
Pinch of sea salt
Vegetable oil for frying
Raw cane sugar
Fresh lemon juice

1. Put the flour and egg into a basin and mix to a stiff paste — don't worry about the lumps at this stage.

2. Gradually add the milk and beat out the lumps.

3. Sprinkle in the salt.

4. Heat the frying pan and pour in a little oil. Add one third of the batter, tilting the pan so that the base is covered.

5. Cook for about 2 minutes then turn it over with a spatula and cook on the other side.

6. Serve immediately, sprinkled with sugar and lemon juice. Roll up or stack to serve.

OTHER BREAKFAST SUGGESTIONS

Cheese on Toast
Toast slices of special gluten-free bread on both sides. Cover one side with thin slices (or grated) Cheddar cheese. Grill for a minute. Put slices of tomato on the cheese and continue grilling until the cheese is bubbly and the tomato cooked.

Bacon and Egg
Grill slices of back bacon. Serve with a poached egg on special gluten-free toast.

Cowboy's Breakfast
Serve slices of grilled back bacon with hot gluten-free baked beans in tomato sauce on special gluten-free toast.

Scrambled Egg
Serve 2 eggs scrambled with a little milk on special gluten-free toast. Garnish with grilled tomatoes or fried mushrooms.

Boiled Egg and Toast Fingers
Lightly boil an egg (3 or 4 minutes). Serve with fingers of buttered special gluten-free toast.

Omelette filled with Fried Mushrooms
Make an omelette with 2 eggs. Fill with 1 oz (50g) mushrooms, fried in a little sunflower oil or similar.

Note: To top up on any of these, serve a gluten-free cereal, milk and raw cane sugar or special gluten-free toast, butter and marmalade.

6.

SNACKS

Snacks may be an important feature of a diet for those who experience a sudden weight loss when they change over from an ordinary diet to a gluten-free one. As all fruit (fresh) is gluten-free, what could be more simple than a piece of fruit as a snack? Bananas are particularly useful and should be regarded as a staple food.

The following recipes are for both sweet and savoury snacks. Biscuits and cookies can be baked in batches and stored in air-tight containers to be used as required. Don't make the mistake of storing biscuits and cookies together as the cookies, being moist, will soften the biscuits. Any biscuits which do go soft in storage can easily be recrisped in the oven for a few minutes.

Sandwiches

As most commercial spreads contain gluten you will need to fall back on home-made spreads and sandwich fillings. One consolation about this situation is that at least you will know exactly what you are eating!

Use special gluten-free bread (see recipe), cut thinly and spread with margarine on one side. Spread one slice or lay on a filling and press the other slice on top. Cut off the crusts for a luxury sandwich. Open sandwiches need only the bottom slice of bread and can be decorated or garnished to look attractive. Unless very easy to manage serve these with a knife and fork.

Fillings/Spreads: always make freshly as you need them.

1. Cottage cheese and chopped dates (not too many) — this makes a very moist sandwich.

2. Hard-boiled egg, chopped and mixed with cress or watercress, finely chopped. This will give you a pale green filling which looks more interesting than most. Season with sea salt and black pepper. Best with brown special gluten-free bread (see recipe).

3. Tinned fish (in *oil*), drained and mashed with chopped hard-boiled egg and a little tomato *purée* (paste).

4. Thin slices of tomato, seasoned with sea salt and a little black pepper, sprinkled with a little raw cane sugar and a few chopped chives.

HAMBURGERS

Imperial (Metric)	American
4 oz (100g) lean minced beef	²⁄₃ cupful lean minced beef
1 thin slice special gluten-free bread (see recipe), made into crumbs	1 thin slice special gluten-free bread (see recipe), made into crumbs
½ a beaten egg	½ a beaten egg
Sea salt and freshly ground black pepper	Sea salt and freshly ground black pepper
1 scant teaspoonful gluten-free soy sauce	1 scant teaspoonful gluten-free soy sauce
½ a small onion, peeled and finely chopped	½ a small onion, peeled and finely chopped
Ground brown rice	Ground brown rice
Vegetable oil for frying	Vegetable oil for frying

1. Put all the ingredients, except the last two, into a basin and mix well.

2. Shape by hand into 2 flat cakes.

3. Dip the burgers in the ground rice to give a thin coating.

4. Fry in shallow hot oil, turning once, for 3 to 4 minutes on each side.

5. Serve between slices of toasted special gluten-free bread (see recipes).

Note: These can be made in advance and stored in the fridge between two plates for a few hours until required.

PIZZA

Imperial (Metric)	American
2 oz (50g) *Trufree* No. 4 flour	1/2 cupful *Trufree* No. 4 flour
3 pinches of sea salt	3 pinches of sea salt
1/2 teaspoonful cream of tartar	1/2 teaspoonful cream of tartar
1/2 teaspoonful bicarbonate of soda	1/2 teaspoonful baking soda
1/2 oz (15g) polyunsaturated soft margarine	1 tablespoonful polyunsaturated soft margarine
1 1/2 tablespoonsful cold water	1 1/2 tablespoonsful cold water
Vegetable oil	Vegetable oil
Topping (from suggestions below)	Topping (from suggestions below)

1. Preheat oven at 425°F/220°C (Gas Mark 7).

2. Put the first 4 ingredients into a basin and mix well.

3. Rub in the margarine and add the water.

4. Mix and knead to a soft dough, using a little more of the flour.

5. Put the dough on to a greased baking sheet and roll or press out into a flat circle.

6. Brush with oil and then arrange the chosen topping.

7. Bake on the top shelf for about 15 minutes and serve hot.

Toppings:

a. Sliced tomato, grated cheese and 2 or 3 black olives;

b. Sliced tomato, fried mushrooms and grated cheese;

c. Sliced tomato, diced ham (without breadcrumb coating) and grated cheese.

As most commercial biscuits are made with wheat, you will need to make your own biscuits at home.

CINNAMON THINS

Imperial (Metric)	American
1 oz (25g) polyunsaturated soft margarine	2½ tablespoonsful polyunsaturated soft margarine
2 tablespoonsful black treacle	2½ tablespoonsful molasses
1 oz (25g) raw cane sugar	2½ tablespoonsful raw cane sugar
3 oz (75g) *Trufree* No. 7 S.R. flour	⅓ cupful *Trufree* No. 7 S.R. flour
½ teaspoonful cinnamon	½ teaspoonful cinnamon

1. Preheat oven at 375°F/190°C (Gas Mark 5).

2. Melt the first 3 ingredients in a saucepan. Cool for 2 minutes.

3. Sift in the flour and cinnamon and mix well.

4. Liberally grease some baking sheets. Put teaspoonsful of the mixture on to the baking sheets, leaving plenty of space around each one as they will spread a good deal during baking.

5. Flatten slightly with a knife and bake above the centre of the oven until brown.

6. Leave the biscuits on the baking sheets to cool for a minute and then loosen and lift them off carefully with a spatula.

7. Cool on a wire rack. As they cool down they will go crisp. (Do not overbake or they will be too crumbly.)

SPICED CURRANT COOKIES

Imperial (Metric)	American
2 oz (50g) polyunsaturated soft margarine	¼ cupful polyunsaturated soft margarine
4 oz (100g) ground brown rice	½ cupful ground brown rice
3 oz (75g) finely grated eating apple	1 small apple, finely grated
1½ oz (40g) raw cane sugar	¼ cupful raw cane sugar
½ teaspoonful gluten-free mixed spice	½ teaspoonful gluten-free mixed spice
1½ oz (40g) currants	¼ cupful currants

1. Preheat oven at 450°F/230°C (Gas Mark 8).

2. In a bowl, blend the margarine and ground rice with a fork.

3. Add the apple, sugar, spice and currants. Knead and mix with a wooden spoon until one large ball of dough is formed.

4. Grease a baking sheet and put 8 to 10 spoonsful of the dough on to it. Spread out into cookie shapes with a knife.

5. Bake for about 20 to 25 minutes.

6. Allow the cookies to cool on a baking sheet, then remove them with a spatula and allow to cool on a wire rack. (The cookies will go crisp as they cool down.)

Note: Eat within 48 hours of baking.

NUT BROWNIES

Imperial (Metric)	**American**
1 egg white	1 egg white
2½ oz (65g) raw cane sugar	½ cupful less 1 tablespoonful raw cane sugar
2½ oz (65g) ground nuts — almonds, hazelnuts, walnuts or mixed nuts	½ cupful plus 1 tablespoonful ground nuts — almonds, hazelnuts, English walnuts or mixed nuts
1 tablespoonful ground brown rice	1 tablespoonful ground brown rice
Grated rind of ½ an orange	Grated rind of ½ an orange
Rice paper	Rice paper

1. Preheat oven at 350°F/180°C (Gas Mark 4).

2. Whisk the egg white until stiff.

3. Add the sugar and nuts.

4. Stir in the ground rice and orange rind.

5. Roll into rounds and place on a baking sheet lined with rice paper, with plenty of space between them.

6. Bake on the centre shelf for 20 to 25 minutes.

7. Allow to grow almost cold and then take them off the baking sheet.

8. Trim off the surplus rice paper with kitchen scissors.

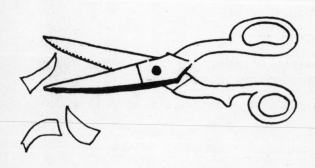

APRICOT JAM COOKIES

Imperial (Metric)
2 oz (50g) polyunsaturated soft margarine
3 oz (75g) raw cane sugar
½ a beaten egg
3 drops of pure vanilla essence
4½ oz (115g) *Trufree* No. 7 S.R. flour
1 oz (25g) shelled almonds, coarsely ground
2 tablespoonsful raw sugar apricot jam

American
¼ cupful polyunsaturated soft margarine
½ cupful raw cane sugar
½ a beaten egg
3 drops of pure vanilla essence
½ cupful plus 1 tablespoonful *Trufree* No. 7 S.R. flour
¼ cupful shelled almonds, coarsely ground
2½ tablespoonsful raw sugar apricot jelly

1. Preheat oven at 375°F/190°C (Gas Mark 5).

2. Cream the margarine and sugar until light.

3. Beat in the egg and almond essence, then add the flour.

4. Use both hands to roll the dough into about 15 balls and roll each one in the almonds.

5. Place them on a well greased baking sheet, spaced well apart to allow them to spread.

6. Use your thumb to make a deep dent in the centre of each cookie.

7. Fill the dents with apricot jam (jelly) (not too much), using a teaspoon.

8. Bake for about 15 minutes, above centre of oven.

9. Leave on the baking sheet for about 5 minutes, then transfer to a wire rack to cool completely.

Note: Don't be too generous with the jam (jelly) or it will bubble over.

GINGER NUTS

Imperial (Metric)	American
4 oz (100g) *Trufree* No. 7 S.R. flour	½ cupful *Trufree* No. 7 S.R. flour
1 teaspoonful dried ginger	1 teaspoonful dried ginger
3 pinches of powdered cloves	3 pinches of powdered cloves
1 oz (25g) polyunsaturated soft margarine	2½ tablespoonsful polyunsaturated soft margarine
2 oz (50g) raw cane sugar	⅓ cupful raw cane sugar
½ a beaten egg	½ a beaten egg
2 tablespoonsful black treacle	2½ tablespoonsful molasses

1. Preheat oven at 350°F/180°C (Gas Mark 4).

2. Put the flour, ginger and ground cloves into a basin and mix well.

3. Beat the margarine to a light cream.

4. Add the sugar and beat again.

5. Beat in the egg and treacle.

6. Add the dry ingredients and mix to a smooth paste.

7. Knead, using more flour, and roll between the palms into about 16 balls.

8. Put on to greased baking sheets and flatten to about 2 in. (50cm) in diameter.

9. Bake for 12 to 15 minutes, above centre of oven.

10. Cool on a wire rack.

PLAIN BISCUITS

Imperial (Metric)	American
2 oz (50g) polyunsaturated soft margarine	¼ cupful polyunsaturated soft margarine
2 oz (50g) raw cane sugar	⅓ cupful raw cane sugar
1 egg	1 egg
½ lb (¼ kilo) *Trufree* No. 7 S.R. flour	1 cupful *Trufree* No. 7 S.R. flour

1. Preheat oven at 400°F/200°C (Gas Mark 6).

2. Cream the margarine and sugar.

3. Beat in the egg.

4. Add the flour and mix into one ball of dough.

5. Knead, using more of the flour, and a little cold water if too stiff.

6. Roll out the dough thinly and cut into about 20 biscuits.

7. Use a spatula to place them on ungreased baking sheets.

8. Prick the biscuits with a fork and bake on the top shelf for about 15 minutes. The biscuits should be pale gold.

9. Cool on a wire rack.

NIBBLES

Most party or cocktails titbits contain gluten so you will need to make your own. It is perhaps easier to make up little dishes with naturally gluten-free items rather than to spend ages in the kitchen baking up curious items!

Here is a list of possibles: radishes, small whole tomatoes, spring onions (scallions) — for non-sensitive tummies, celery stalks, all kinds of nuts, sunflower seeds, raisins, dried apricots and sultanas (golden seedless raisins). Remember: fresh fruit is all gluten-free.

HOT JAM SANDWICH

This is rather like a giant doughnut and looks and tastes delicious. For each sandwich you will need two slices of fairly thick bread (special), margarine, raw sugar jam (jelly) and raw cane sugar.

Heat margarine in a frying pan and fry each slice of bread on one side only, until crisp and golden. Sprinkle a little raw cane sugar on a warm plate and lay one of the slices on it, fried side down. Spread with raw sugar jam (jelly) and cover with the other slice of bread so that the fried side is uppermost. Sprinkle with a little more sugar and serve right away with a spoon.

7.

SOUPS AND STARTERS

Home-made soups are always far superior to the commercial ones.
Serve as a snack or with a meal. Pack in a thermos for picnic meals.
   Traditional soup recipes will not need many alterations to make
them gluten-free. Take care with thickenings and stock. Do not add
any kind of noodles unless gluten-free (special) ones. Use freshly
ground black pepper instead of white pepper.

SPLIT PEA SOUP

Imperial (Metric)	American
½ lb (¼ kilo) dried split peas	1 cupful dried split peas
1 large or 2 small onions, peeled and sliced	1 large or 2 small onions, peeled and sliced
1 tablespoonful vegetable oil	1 tablespoonful vegetable oil
1 pint (½ litre) water	2½ cupsful water
1 tablespoonful thin, gluten-free soy sauce	1 tablespoonful thin, gluten-free soy sauce
½ lb (¼ kilo) carrots, trimmed, scrubbed and sliced	8 ounces carrots, trimmed, scrubbed and sliced
Sea salt and freshly ground black pepper	Sea salt and freshly ground black pepper

1. Put the split peas into a fine mesh sieve and wash them under the cold tap.

2. Put the peas into a large bowl with well over 1 pint (½ litre) of water and leave overnight to swell.

3. Fry the onion in the oil for 3 or 4 minutes. Pour in the fresh water and the soy sauce.

4. Strain the soaked peas and add them to the saucepan with the carrots and a sprinkling of salt. Bring to the boil and simmer gently with the lid on for 1 to 1¼ hours, stirring from time to time. (If the soup thickens too much, add more water.)

5. Season to taste and serve hot.

Note: This is a very nourishing and filling soup. Serve with brown special bread or special sippets (see page 54).

WINTER VEGETABLE SOUP

Imperial (Metric)	American
1 medium-sized onion, peeled and sliced	1 medium-sized onion, peeled and sliced
1 tablespoonful thin vegetable oil	1 tablespoonful thin vegetable oil
1 medium-sized carrot, scrubbed and sliced thinly	1 medium-sized carrot, scrubbed and sliced thinly
1 small parsnip, peeled and sliced	1 small parsnip, peeled and sliced
1 small turnip, peeled and sliced	1 small turnip, peeled and sliced
4 sprouts, trimmed and sliced	4 sprouts, trimmed and sliced
1 medium-sized potato, peeled and sliced	1 medium-sized potato, peeled and sliced
1 pint (½ litre) water	2½ cupsful water
1 tablespoonful gluten-free soy sauce	1 tablespoonful gluten-free soy sauce
Sea salt and freshly ground black pepper	Sea salt and freshly ground black pepper

1. Fry the onion in the oil.

2. Put in the rest of the vegetables and about half the water.

3. Bring to the boil and then simmer with the lid on for about 20 minutes.

4. Add the rest of the water to cool it down, then liquidize.

5. Return the soup to the pan and add the soy sauce and seasoning to taste.

6. Serve hot.

Variation: Just before serving, add 1 heaped tablespoonful of freshly chopped parsley.

FRENCH ONION SOUP
(2 servings)

Imperial (Metric)	American
1 large onion	1 large onion
½ oz (15g) polyunsaturated soft margarine	1 tablespoonful polyunsaturated soft margarine
1 heaped teaspoonful maize flour	1 heaped teaspoonful cornmeal
¾ pint (400ml) water	2 cupsful water
Seasoning to taste	Seasoning to taste
2 teaspoonsful gluten-free soy sauce	2 teaspoonsful gluten-free soy sauce
2 slices special gluten-free bread (see recipes), toasted	2 slices special gluten-free bread (see recipes), toasted
2 oz (50g) grated cheese	½ cupful grated cheese

1. Peel the onion and chop it finely.

2. Melt the margarine in a saucepan and cook the onion in this until transparent.

3. Stir the maize flour (cornmeal) into the water and pour it into the saucepan. Mix well.

4. Bring to the boil then lower the heat and simmer for about 25 minutes, adding the seasoning and the soy sauce.

5. Serve hot poured over the toast cut into cubes and sprinkled with the cheese.

CELERY SOUP
(2 servings)

Imperial (Metric)

½ a medium-sized onion, peeled and sliced

2 teaspoonsful thin vegetable oil

2-3 stalks of celery, including leaves, washed and chopped small

¼ pint (150ml) water

2 scant teaspoonsful gluten-free soy sauce

Sea salt and freshly ground black pepper

American

½ a medium-sized onion, peeled and sliced

2 teaspoonsful thin vegetable oil

2-3 stalks of celery, including leaves, washed and chopped small

⅔ cupful water

2 scant teaspoonsful gluten-free soy sauce

Sea salt and freshly ground black pepper

1. Fry the onion in the oil until transparent.

2. Add the celery and stir-fry with the onion for 3 or 4 minutes.

3. Liquidize with the water.

4. Pour the soup back into the saucepan, bring to the boil, then simmer for 5 minutes.

5. Pour into a jug and strain back into the saucepan through a fine mesh sieve.

6. Add the soy sauce and seasoning.

7. Leave to stand for a few hours, then reheat and serve.

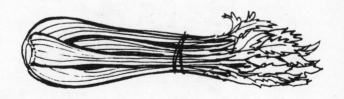

PARSLEY SOUP — COLD
(3 servings)

Imperial (Metric)	American
1 small onion, peeled and sliced thinly	1 small onion, peeled and sliced thinly
1 tablespoonful vegetable oil	1 tablespoonful vegetable oil
2 medium-sized potatoes, peeled and sliced thinly	2 medium-sized potatoes, peeled and sliced thinly
2 oz (50g) fresh parsley, washed and chopped	2 cupsful fresh parsley, washed and chopped
3 teaspoonsful gluten-free soy sauce	3 teaspoonsful gluten-free soy sauce
1 pint (½ litre) water	2½ cupsful water
Sea salt and freshly ground black pepper	Sea salt and freshly ground black pepper

1. Fry the onion in the oil for 3 to 4 minutes with the lid on.

2. Add the potato slices and chopped parsley. Stir and add the soy sauce and water. Bring to the boil and simmer with the lid on for half an hour.

3. Remove from the heat and allow to cool for a few minutes. Liquidize in a blender and return to the saucepan.

4. Taste and season. Dilute with more water if you think it is too thick.

5. Allow to cool. Pour into a jug and place in the fridge for at least an hour. Serve cold from the fridge.

WATERCRESS SOUP
(3 servings)

Imperial (Metric)
1 medium-sized onion, peeled and sliced finely
2 teaspoonsful vegetable oil
1 medium-sized cold boiled potato
1 bunch watercress (including stems), washed thoroughly and coarsely chopped
¾ pint (400ml) water
2-3 teaspoonsful gluten-free soy sauce
Sea salt

American
1 medium-sized onion, peeled and sliced finely
2 teaspoonsful vegetable oil
1 medium-sized cold boiled potato
1 bunch watercress (including stems), washed thoroughly and coarsely chopped
2 cupsful water
2-3 teaspoonsful gluten-free soy sauce
Sea salt

1. Fry the onion in the oil until transparent but not brown.

2. Put the onion, potato, watercress and about half the water into the liquidizer. Blend and pour into the saucepan.

3. Add the remaining water and the soy sauce. Bring to the boil and simmer for 10 minutes.

4. Season to taste and serve hot or cold.

ONION AND TOMATO SOUP
(2-3 servings)

Imperial (Metric)
2 medium-sized onions
1 oz (25g) polyunsaturated soft
  margarine
1 medium-sized tin tomatoes
1 teaspoonful raw cane sugar
2 teaspoonful gluten-free soy sauce
Sea salt and freshly ground black
  pepper

American
2 medium-sized onions
2½ tablespoonsful polyunsaturated
  soft margarine
1 medium-sized can tomatoes
1 teaspoonful raw cane sugar
2 teaspoonsful gluten-free soy sauce
Sea salt and freshly ground black
  pepper

1. Fry the onion in the margarine until it is transparent.

2. Liquidize the tomatoes with the cooked onion and return to the
    saucepan.

3. Add the sugar, soy sauce and seasoning.

4. Bring to the boil and simmer while stirring.

5. Serve hot, diluted with water if preferred.

MUSHROOM SOUP
(2 servings)

Imperial (Metric)
1/2 a medium-sized onion, peeled and sliced
2 teaspoonsful vegetable oil
2 oz (50g) fresh mushrooms, washed and sliced
1/2 pint (1/4 litre) water
1-2 teaspoonsful gluten-free soy sauce
Sea salt and freshly ground black pepper

American
1/2 a medium-sized onion, peeled and sliced
2 teaspoonsful vegetable oil
1 cupful fresh mushrooms, washed and sliced
1 1/3 cupsful water
1-2 teaspoonsful gluten-free soy sauce
Sea salt and freshly ground black pepper

1. Fry the onion in the oil for 3 to 4 minutes.

2. Place the fried onions, mushroom slices, water and soy sauce in a liquidizer. Blend and pour back into the saucepan.

3. Bring to the boil and simmer for about 5 minutes.

4. Season to taste and serve hot.

SIPPETS

Fry cubes of special gluten-free bread lightly in hot vegetable oil until golden. Sprinkle into hot soup and serve. (Cut the bread into thick slices and then into cubes.)

HOT GRAPEFRUIT
(Serves 1)

Imperial (Metric)	American
½ a grapefruit	½ a grapefruit
Raw cane sugar	Raw cane sugar
Polyunsaturated soft margarine	Polyunsaturated soft margarine

1. Loosen the flesh of the grapefruit all round with a sharp knife, and also cut between the segments.

2. Place the grapefruit in the grill pan and sprinkle with a little sugar.

3. Put a small knob of the special margarine in the centre and grill until it begins to brown.

4. Serve immediately in a rounded bowl with a teaspoon.

LIVER PÂTÉ

Imperial (Metric)	American
½ lb (¼ kilo) chicken livers	8 ounces chicken livers
Sea salt and freshly ground black pepper	Sea salt and freshly ground black pepper
1 small onion or shallot, peeled and chopped very finely	1 small onion or shallot, peeled and chopped very finely
1 oz (25g) polyunsaturated soft margarine or 1 tablespoonful vegetable oil	2½ tablespoonsful polyunsaturated soft margarine or 1 tablespoonful vegetable oil
3 good pinches of dried mixed herbs	3 good pinches of dried mixed herbs
1 small clove garlic, peeled	1 small clove garlic, peeled
1 teaspoonful sherry or white wine	1 teaspoonful sherry or white wine

1. Wash the livers and cut out stringy parts and yellow pieces.

2. Dry thoroughly and chop into small pieces. Sprinkle with salt and pepper.

3. Fry the chopped onion in the margarine or oil, using a small saucepan.

4. Add the chopped liver and herbs, and crush in the garlic through a garlic press.

5. Turn up the heat a little and stir with a small wooden spoon. The liver will start to crumble and turn a pinky-brown colour. This should take about 5 minutes. Mash with a fork to a smooth paste.

6. Add the sherry or white wine. Stir, taste and correct seasoning.

7. Allow the pâté to cool, then place it in little dishes and cover with a foil lid. Store in the fridge and eat within 3 days.

8. Serve with hot gluten-free toast or as a spread in sandwiches made with gluten-free bread (see recipes). Garnish with parsley.

CRUDITÉS

Served as dips with special mayonnaise (page 57), these make an ideal starter.

Radishes — scrubbed and trimmed.

Celery — scrubbed and trimmed and cut into short lengths.

Carrot — washed and trimmed and cut into matchstick shapes.

Spring Onion (Scallion) — washed and trimmed.

Cauliflower — use the crisp, white florets after washing well.

Lettuce — use just the heart leaves. Wash and pat dry with a clean tea-towel. (Any variety of lettuce will do.)

Tomato — only use if you can get small fruits. Wash and leave whole.

MAYONNAISE

Imperial (Metric)	American
1 tablespoonful ground brown rice	1 tablespoonful ground brown rice
8 tablespoonsful water	10 tablespoonsful water
2 tablespoonsful soya flour	2½ tablespoonsful soya flour
3 tablespoonsful wine or cider vinegar	3½ tablespoonsful wine or cider vinegar
8 tablespoonsful sunflower oil or similar	10 tablespoonsful sunflower oil or similar
3 teaspoonsful raw cane sugar	3 teaspoonsful raw cane sugar
1 teaspoonful sea salt	1 teaspoonful sea salt
1 teaspoonful gluten-free ready-made mustard (usually French is suitable)	1 teaspoonful gluten-free ready-made mustard (usually French is suitable)

1. Place the ground rice in a small saucepan with the water and cook while you stir for about 4 minutes. The mixture should be smooth and thick.

2. Leave to cool.

3. Press the soya flour with the back of a spoon to remove any lumps.

4. Put into a liquidizer with the rest of the ingredients and blend to a cream.

5. Store covered in the fridge for up to a week. Use as required.

PRAWN COCKTAIL

Imperial (Metric)
1 lettuce leaf
½ a medium-sized tomato
1 oz (25g) peeled prawns
1 tablespoonful special mayonnaise
  (page 57)
½ teaspoonful tomato *purée*
4 or 5 drops of lemon juice
3 or 4 pinches of raw cane sugar
Sea salt and freshly ground black
  pepper

American
1 lettuce leaf
½ a medium-sized tomato
2½ tablespoonsful peeled prawns
1 tablespoonful special mayonnaise
  (page 57)
½ teaspoonful tomato paste
4 or 5 drops of lemon juice
3 or 4 pinches of raw cane sugar
Sea salt and freshly ground black
  pepper

1. Tear the lettuce leaf into small pieces and put into a glass dish.

2. Cover with the tomato, cut into wedges.

3. Place the prawns on top.

4. Put the mayonnaise into a cup with the tomato *purée* (paste) and mix.

5. Add the lemon juice and the sugar. Stir well.

6. Taste and season with salt and pepper. Pour or spoon the dressing over the prawns.

Note: This is usually served with brown bread and butter. Use special gluten-free brown bread (page 22).

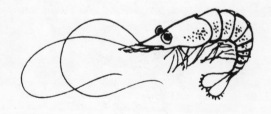

MUSHROOMS À LA GRECQUE
(4 servings)

Imperial (Metric)	American
1 medium-sized onion, grated	1 medium-sized onion, grated
2 tablespoonsful sunflower oil or similar	2½ tablespoonsful sunflower oil or similar
1 wineglassful dry white wine	1 wineglassful dry white wine
1 small clove garlic, peeled	1 small clove garlic, peeled
¾ lb (350g) button mushrooms	6 cupsful button mushrooms
4 medium-sized fresh tomatoes	4 medium-sized fresh tomatoes
Sea salt and freshly ground black pepper	Sea salt and freshly ground black pepper
Freshly chopped parsley	Freshly chopped parsley

1. Fry the onion in the oil, but do not let it brown.

2. Add the wine and crush in the garlic through a garlic press.

3. Wash the mushrooms and leave them whole.

4. Stab each tomato with a fork and plunge into boiling water. As they split, remove and peel them. Cut into quarters.

5. Put the mushrooms and tomato quarters into the onion mixture. Cook for about 10 minutes until the liquid has halved in quantity.

6. Season to taste and leave to grow cold. Chill in the fridge and serve in small dishes with a sprinkling of parsley. At the same time, serve fingers of special gluten-free toast and margarine or butter.

Variation: If you do not want to make this with white wine, use a non-fizzy kind of apple juice instead.

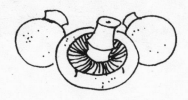

SUGGESTIONS FOR OTHER STARTERS

Melon

Fresh grapefruit with a little raw cane sugar

Mixed grapefruit and orange segments with a little raw cane sugar

Avocado with prawns and special mayonnaise (page 57).

Radishes or tomatoes with special gluten-free bread and butter

Green salad of lettuce (2 kinds), watercress, cucumber, green pepper
    strips etc. Sprinkle with 3 pinches of raw cane sugar, sea salt and
    freshly ground black pepper, 2 teaspoonsful of vegetable oil and
    1 teaspoonful of wine vinegar. Serve in individual bowls.

8

MAIN MEALS

EGG FLORENTINE
(Serves 1)

Imperial (Metric)	American
4 oz (100g) cooked and well drained spinach, chopped small	½ cupful cooked and well drained spinach, chopped small
½ oz (15g) butter or polyunsaturated soft margarine	1 tablespoonful butter or polyunsaturated soft margarine
Grated nutmeg	Grated nutmeg
Sea salt and freshly ground black pepper	Sea salt and freshly ground black pepper
1 egg	1 egg
1 tablespoonful Parmesan cheese	1 tablespoonful Parmesan cheese

1. Heat the spinach with the butter or margarine and sprinkle with a couple of pinches of nutmeg.

2. Put into a small ovenproof dish and make a hollow in the middle.

3. Carefully break the egg into the hollow and sprinkle the cheese over it.

4. Bake in a preheated oven at 350°F/180°C (Gas Mark 4) for about 15 minutes or until the egg is set.

5. Serve with toasted special gluten-free bread.

BAKER'S OMELETTE
3-4 servings

Imperial (Metric)
1 small onion, peeled and chopped
1 tablespoonful sunflower oil
2 boiled potatoes, sliced
2 tomatoes
2 medium-sized mushrooms
1 heaped tablespoonful cooked peas
  or chopped cooked vegetables
6 eggs
Sea salt and freshly ground black
  pepper
1 teaspoonful freshly chopped
  parsley

American
1 small onion, peeled and chopped
1 tablespoonful sunflower oil
2 boiled potatoes, sliced
2 tomatoes
2 medium-sized mushrooms
1 heaped tablespoonful cooked peas
  or chopped cooked vegetables
6 eggs
Sea salt and freshly ground black
  pepper
1 teaspoonful freshly chopped
  parsley

1. Preheat oven at 450°F/220°C (Gas Mark 7) and put in a largish, shallow, ovenproof dish to warm on the top shelf.

2. Fry the onion in the oil for about 5 minutes.

3. Add the vegetables and gently heat through.

4. Transfer to the warmed dish.

5. Beat the eggs in a bowl and season.

6. Pour over the vegetables and bake on the top shelf for about 10 to 15 minutes until the eggs have set.

7. Sprinkle with the chopped parsley and serve hot with a side salad.

This recipe makes enough for 3 or 4 servings, so can be served to the whole family. A very quick and nourishing meal.

COQ AU VIN

Imperial (Metric)

2 slices streaky bacon, derinded and chopped
1 tablespoonful sunflower oil or similar
2 chicken breasts, skinned
2 medium-sized onions
¼ bottle red wine
2 cloves garlic, peeled
1 small bay leaf
Pinch of mixed herbs
Sea salt and freshly ground black pepper
4 medium-sized mushrooms, sliced
1 tablespoonful ground brown rice

American

2 slices streaky bacon, derinded and chopped
1 tablespoonful sunflower oil or similar
2 chicken breasts, skinned
2 medium-sized onions
¼ bottle red wine
2 cloves garlic, peeled
1 small bay leaf
Pinch of mixed herbs
Sea salt and freshly ground black pepper
4 medium-sized mushrooms, sliced
1 tablespoonful ground brown rice

1. Fry the bacon in the oil for a few minutes in a flameproof casserole.

2. Put in the chicken breasts and fry, turning them over to seal.

3. Peel and slice the onions. Add these to the casserole and stir well while frying them for 2 or 3 minutes.

4. Add the wine, crush in the garlic, sprinkle in the herbs and seasoning.

5. Bring to the boil and add the mushrooms. Sprinkle in the ground rice and stir well.

6. Cook in the oven for another 45 minutes at 375°F/190°C (Gas Mark 5).

7. Serve hot with green vegetables and plain boiled brown rice.

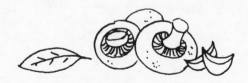

COTTAGE PIE

Imperial (Metric)	American
2 medium-sized onions, sliced	2 medium-sized onions, sliced
2 tablespoonsful vegetable oil	2½ tablespoonsful vegetable oil
1 lb (½ kilo) lean, minced beef	1 pound lean, minced beef
1 tablespoonful ground brown rice	1 tablespoonful ground brown rice
1 heaped teaspoonful tomato *puree*	1 heaped teaspoonful tomato paste
3 teaspoonsful gluten-free soy sauce	3 teaspoonsful gluten-free soy sauce
¼ pint (150ml) water	⅔ cupful water
Sea salt and freshly ground black pepper	Sea salt and freshly ground black pepper
4 portions hot, boiled potatoes	4 portions hot, boiled potatoes
1 oz (25g) polyunsaturated soft margarine	2½ tablespoonsful polyunsaturated soft margarine
A little water	A little water
3 pinches of grated nutmeg	3 pinches of grated nutmeg

1. Preheat oven at 375°F/190°C (Gas Mark 5) and put a casserole in to warm.

2. Fry the onion in the oil for about 5 minutes.

2. Add the beef and fry very gently while stirring for another 5 minutes.

4. Sprinkle in the ground rice and add the tomato *purée* (paste) and soy sauce.

5. Stir well and add enough water to make a sloppy mixture.

6. Season and spoon into the warmed casserole. Put back into the oven to keep warm.

7. Mash the potatoes well, adding the margarine.

8. Pour in a little water and beat with a wooden spoon.

9. Add the nutmeg and season to taste. Give it a final stir and pile on top of the meat mixture, spreading it out evenly over the top with a fork.

10. Bake for about 30 minutes on the middle shelf, then serve hot with green vegetables and carrots.

SPANISH OMELETTE

Imperial (Metric)	American
1 tablespoonful vegetable oil	1 tablespoonful vegetable oil
1 medium-sized boiled potato, cut into thick slices	1 medium-sized boiled potato, cut into thick slices
1 small onion	1 small onion
Small piece green or red pepper, cut into strips	Small piece green or red pepper, cut into strips
2 medium-sized tomatoes, sliced	2 medium-sized tomatoes, sliced
½ small clove garlic, peeled	½ small clove garlic, peeled
2 eggs	2 eggs
1 teaspoonful cold water	1 teaspoonful cold water
Sea salt and freshly ground black pepper	Sea salt and freshly ground black pepper

1. Put the oil into a heavy-based frying pan.

2. Heat the potato slices and the onion, peeled and sliced finely.

3. Fry, turning once, for about a minute on each side.

4. Add the strips of pepper and the tomatoes. Crush in the garlic and distribute it in the pan.

5. Beat the eggs lightly with the water and when you think the pan is hot enough, pour over the cooked mixture. Cook for a minute or two until the eggs have set.

6. Season to taste and loosen the omelette with a spatula. Serve immediately on a hot plate with a green side-salad.

Note: A good quick meal that makes the minimum of washing-up! Some people prefer it without the pepper (green or red) as they find it rather indigestible.

TROUT WITH ALMONDS

Imperial (Metric)	American
1 trout, cleaned but with head and tail left on	1 trout, cleaned but with head and tail left on
Sea salt and freshly ground black pepper	Sea salt and freshly ground black pepper
Generous knob of polyunsaturated soft margarine	Generous knob of polyunsaturated soft margarine
1 tablespoonful flaked almonds	1 tablespoonful flaked almonds
Juice of ¼ of a fresh lemon	Juice of ¼ of a fresh lemon
Lemon slices and parsley to garnish	Lemon slices and parsley to garnish

1. Wash and dry the fish. Sprinkle with salt and pepper.

2. Melt the margarine in a frying pan and fry the fish for about 6 minutes on each side until golden and cooked through.

3. Take out of the pan carefully and place on a warm plate. Keep the fish hot while you prepare the almonds.

4. Fry the almonds in what is left in the pan. Squeeze in the lemon juice and mix with the almonds.

5. Spoon over the fish and garnish with a lemon slice and a sprig of parsley.

6. Serve with a side-salad or with savoury brown rice.

Note: Be careful when you put in the lemon juice as it will sizzle.

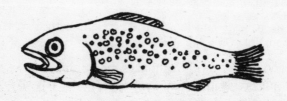

PLAICE WITH CUCUMBER

Imperial (Metric)
1 fillet of plaice
1 tablespoonful ground brown rice
   mixed with 2 pinches of sea salt
1 oz (25g) polyunsaturated soft
   margarine
1½ in. (3.5cm) cucumber, peeled
   and cut into thick slices

American
1 fillet of plaice
1 tablespoonful ground brown rice
   with 2 pinches of sea salt
2½ tablespoonsful polyunsaturated
   soft margarine
1½ in. cucumber, peeled and cut
   into thick slices

1. Put a dinner plate to warm.

2. Wash the plaice fillet and coat with the rice.

3. Put the margarine into a frying pan, heat and use to fry the plaice,
   turning once. This should take about 4 minutes.

4. Take the pan off the heat and remove the fish with a spatula.
   Put on to the warmed plate and keep warm.

5. Add the lemon juice to the pan, stir and return to the heat.

6. Put in the cucumber slices and quickly heat through. Arrange
   them on top of the fish.

7. Serve immediately with carrots, grilled tomatoes or any brightly
   coloured vegetables and plain boiled brown rice.

Note: Seasoning is put on at the table.

FISH CASSEROLE
(Serves 2)

Imperial (Metric)	American
1 medium-sized leek	1 medium-sized leek
1/2 a green pepper, de-seeded	1/2 a green pepper, de-seeded
1 tablespoonful vegetable oil	1 tablespoonful vegetable oil
1/4 pint (150ml) tomato juice	2/3 cupful tomato juice
2 medium-sized tomatoes	2 medium-sized tomatoes
Sea salt and freshly ground black pepper	Sea salt and freshly ground black pepper
8-10 oz (225-300g) haddock or cod fillet	8-10 ounces haddock or cod fillet
1 tablespoonful fresh lemon juice	1 tablespoonful fresh lemon juice
2 heaped teaspoonsful finely chopped fresh parsley	2 heaped teaspoonsful finely chopped fresh parsley

1. Preheat oven at 350°F/180°C (Gas Mark 4).

2. Put in an ovenproof casserole to warm.

3. Prepare the leek and cut into smallish pieces with the green pepper.

4. Heat the oil in a saucepan and stir-fry the vegetables for 7 or 8 minutes until they are tender, adding the tomato juice after 4 minutes.

5. Remove from heat and put in the tomatoes, cut into four.

6. Season and put into the warmed casserole.

7. Cut the fish into two portions and place on top.

8. Pour the lemon juice over the fish and sprinkle with the chopped parsley.

9. Put the lid on the casserole and bake for 15 minutes or a little longer if the fillet is thick.

10. Serve with hot brown rice or plain boiled potatoes.

LAMB WITH HERBS
(Serves 1)

Imperial (Metric)	American
1 or 2 lamb chops	1 or 2 lamb chops
1 clove garlic	1 clove garlic
Dried rosemary	Dried rosemary
Sea salt and freshly ground black pepper	Sea salt and freshly ground black pepper

1. Trim the chops of fat and wash them under the tap. Dry and put into the grill pan on a grid.

2. Cut the clove of garlic in half and rub over the meat.

3. Sprinkle with a little rosemary and seasoning.

4. Grill for about 15 minutes, turning once.

5. Serve at once with boiled potatoes and hot green vegetables. Peas and carrots are especially good with this dish.

GRAVY

Many people believe that gravy can only be made with a stock/gravy cube or a packet mix. This is nonsense. The best gravy is made from the natural stock contained in meat juices, a little thickening such as maize flour (cornmeal) and the strainings from vegetables. A little soy sauce can be added for colouring and extra flavour.

1. Strain the fat off the meat juices from the grill or roasting pan.

2. Sprinkle in about 1-2 heaped teaspoonsful of maize flour (cornmeal) and rub it into the juices with a wooden spoon.

3. While you heat, gradually add the strainings from any vegetables you have cooked, and 1-2 teaspoonsful of gluten-free soy sauce.

4. Stir while it thickens and serve hot with the meat and vegetables. If it turns out lumpy, then strain before using.

Variation: Use half a boiled and well mashed potato as a thickener instead of the maize flour (cornmeal).

Note: It is important to strain off all the fat from the meat juices or the gravy will be far too greasy.

LIVER WITH ORANGE

Imperial (Metric)	American
2 oz (50g) lamb's liver	1 medium-sized piece lamb's liver
1 tablespoonful vegetable oil	1 tablespoonful vegetable oil
½ a peeled orange, cut into slices	½ peeled orange, cut into slices
2 teaspoonsful gluten-free soy sauce	2 teaspoonsful gluten-free soy sauce
1 tablespoonful pure orange juice	1 tablespoonful pure orange juice

1. Cut out any stringy pieces from the liver. Wash, dry and cut it into small pieces.

2. Heat the oil in a frying pan and put in the liver. Fry gently while turning to cook evenly for 5 minutes.

3. Add the orange slices, soy sauce and orange juice. Heat through gently.

4. Serve hot with green vegetables and either plain boiled brown rice or potatoes.

Variation: If you prefer a thicker gravy, dip the liver pieces in maize flour (cornmeal) before frying. (Seasoning is added at the table.)

COLD MEAT AND SALADS

Beef, lamb and pork slices cut off a cold joint roasted the day before make an easy meal with salad and jacket potatoes. Here are some salad suggestions and instructions for the jacket potatoes.

RED SALAD
(Serves 4)

The colour of this salad is simply amazing!

Imperial (Metric)	American
3 oz (75g) red pepper	½ cupful red pepper, cut into strips
6 oz (150g) red cabbage	1 cupful red cabbage, shredded
4 oz (100g) carrot	1 cupful carrot, grated
4 oz (100g) fresh tomato	1 cupful fresh tomato, chopped
4 oz (100g) raw beetroot	1 cupful beet, grated

1. Wash and prepare the vegetables.

2. Cut the red pepper into strips.

3. Shred the red cabbage finely.

4. Grate the carrot.

5. Cut the tomato into small pieces.

6. Grate the beetroot coarsely.

7. Combine all the ingredients in a bowl and dress lightly before serving with an oil and vinegar dressing and a seasoning of sea salt and black pepper.

Variation: For a slightly sweet salad sprinkle a little raw cane sugar over the finished salad. (This is especially good with cold pork or ham.)

GREEN SALAD
There are several types of greens, other than lettuce, that can be used for a green salad. Any mixture of the following on a base of either lettuce or cabbage will make an excellent salad.

Watercress — washed very carefully. Discard tougher stems and any discoloured leaves. Tear into sprigs.

Cress or Mustard Greens — cut off as near to the roots as you can and rinse in a colander under the cold tap.

Cabbage — choose heart leaves that will not be too tough. Wash and trim coarse stalks away. Shred finely.

Spinach — use young, tender leaves. Cut out coarse stalks. Tear the leaves into small pieces.

Kale — use only tender leaves. Wash well and tear or cut into small pieces.

Brussels Sprouts — trim, wash and shred finely.

Lettuce — wash leaves well and pat dry with a clean tea-towel. Tear into pieces.

Sliced spring onions (scallions) or the ordinary type of onion (chopped or sliced into rings) can also be used in a green salad; cucumber and finely chopped fresh parsley also make useful garnishes. Serve with an oil and vinegar dressing, but first sprinkle the mixed salad with a few pinches of raw cane sugar, sea salt and freshly ground black pepper.

OIL AND VINEGAR DRESSING
Put 1 tablespoonful of wine or cider vinegar and 3 tablespoonsful (3½ US) of sunflower oil into a screw-top jar. Shake well before using. (This dressing should be used to moisten salads not to swamp them.)

JACKET POTATOES
Choose old potatoes and scrub with a hard brush to remove any dirt. Cut out any 'eyes' or discoloured parts with a sharp knife. Pierce the skin with the point of the knife in several places. (This is to let out steam during baking.) Put a metal skewer through the centre of each one and place on a baking sheet. Bake in a preheated oven at 425°F/220°C (Gas Mark 7) for about an hour or until the flesh is soft. Eat the whole potato including the skin and serve with polyunsaturated soft margarine.

STIR-FRY VEGETABLES

This is a quick method of partly cooking vegetables so that they are just soft enough to eat. Use a large flat pan with sloping sides. Prepare a mixed selection of vegetables, cutting them into small pieces or thin slices (root vegetables). Always start with a sliced onion and a tablespoonful of sunflower oil. Stir while you fry this for 3 minutes. Now add the rest of the vegetables in order of hardness, carrot first, cucumber and tomato last. As you put them in, use the middle of the pan and keep turning them over. Push the cooked vegetables to the side of the pan and the raw ones into the middle. Add a sprinkling of sea salt and a tablespoonful or two of water. Mix a little gluten-free soy sauce with the juices and you have a lovely gravy. What could be easier?

SAVOURY RICE

Imperial (Metric)	American
1 medium-sized onion, peeled and chopped	1 medium-sized onion, peeled and chopped
1 tablespoonful sunflower oil or similar	1 tablespoonful sunflower oil or similar
½ green pepper, de-seeded and chopped	½ a green pepper, de-seeded and chopped
1 carrot, scrubbed and chopped	1 carrot, scrubbed and chopped
1 stalk of celery, washed and chopped	1 stalk of celery, washed and chopped
3 Brussels sprouts or 2 tender cabbage or spinach leaves, shredded after trimming	3 Brussels sprouts or 2 tender cabbage or spinach leaves, shredded after trimming
1 portion cooked brown rice	1 portion cooked brown rice
Sea salt and freshly ground black pepper to taste	Sea salt and freshly ground black pepper to taste
Squeeze of lemon juice (optional)	Squeeze of lemon juice (optional)

1. Fry the onion gently in the oil for a few minutes.

2. Add the prepared vegetables and a little water to prevent sticking.

3. Cook with the lid on tightly for about 6 or 7 minutes.

4. Add the cooked rice and mix everything together. Cook until the rice has heated through.

5. Season and add the lemon juice, if liked.

6. Serve hot with fish or meat.

Variation: Other kinds of vegetables can be used according to season — green beans, peas, turnips, parsnips, broad beans (Windsor beans) etc. If you want to use tomato this is best served as a garnish as it is very soft when cooked and tends to make the dish too moist.

BASIC SAVOURY SAUCE MIX

Imperial (Metric)	American
1 tablespoonful butter or margarine	1 slightly heaped tablespoonful
½ oz (15g) gluten-free maize flour	butter or margarine
½ pint (¼ litre) milk	1 tablespoonful cornmeal
Flavouring from following list	1⅓ cupsful milk
Sea salt and freshly ground black	Flavouring from following list
pepper	Sea salt and freshly ground black
	pepper

1. Melt the margarine in a saucepan.

2. Blend the mazie flour (cornmeal) and milk in a bowl, stirring out any lumps.

3. Pour this into the pan with the margarine and stir well.

4. Add the flavouring of your choice.

5. Heat through and simmer for about 3 minutes, stirring all the time while the mixture cooks.

6. Serve hot, immediately, on vegetables or fish.

FLAVOURINGS

PARSLEY — add one or two level teaspoonsful freshly chopped parsley.

MUSHROOM — add 2 oz (50g) fried mushrooms, chopped very finely.

ONION — add one small onion, fried in a little sunflower oil until soft. Chop the onion very finely before frying.

TOMATO — add one tablespoonful tomato *purée* (gluten-free). Stir in well.

CHEESE — add 1 to 2 oz (25-50g) ¼-½ cupful grated hard cheese or Parmesan cheese. Cook the sauce while stirring until all the cheese has melted.

Serve any one of these savoury sauces poured over baked, poached or steamed fish. Serve with a green vegetable such as peas and potatoes or rice, plain boiled.

CAULIFLOWER CHEESE

Pour hot cheese sauce over plain boiled or steamed cauliflower.
Sprinkle a little more cheese on top and brown under the grill for
a few minutes. The cauliflower should be tender but not soft as this
will spoil the dish. Serve with special gluten-free bread and butter
or margarine.

LEEKS IN CHEESE SAUCE

Imperial (Metric)	American
1 portion prepared leeks (generous)	1 portion prepared leeks (generous)
1 hard boiled egg	1 hard boiled egg
Cheese sauce	Cheese sauce
Grated cheese for topping	Grated cheese for topping

1. Cook the leeks, cut into short lengths, in boiling salted water until
   tender.

2. Strain well and put into an ovenproof dish.

3. Peel the hard boiled egg. Slice and lay on top of the leeks.

4. Cover with cheese sauce.

5. Sprinkle top with grated cheese and grill until bubbling and just
   beginning to brown.

6. Serve hot with special gluten-free bread and butter or margarine.

PASTA
3-4 servings

Imperial (Metric)	American
8 oz (¼ kilo) *Trufree* No. 4 flour	1 cupful *Trufree* No. 4 flour
3 pinches sea salt	3 pinches sea salt
2 tablespoonsful sunflower oil	2½ tablespoonsful sunflower oil
1 egg, beaten	1 egg, beaten
3 tablespoonsful cold water	3½ tablespoonsful cold water

1. Put the flour and salt into a bowl and mix.

2. Add the oil and rub in with the fingers.

3. Put in the beaten egg and mix.

4. Add the water and mix to a sticky paste.

5. Knead, using more of the flour if you need to, until smooth.

6. Divide the dough into 4 portions and roll out each portion on a floured worktop, as thin as you can.

7. Cut into narrow strips with a sharp knife.

To Cook Pasta
1. Heat a large pan of water to which a sprinkle of sea salt has been added.

2. Drop in the raw pasta and bring to the boil.

3. Cook steadily for about 12 minutes, until the pasta is tender but still firm.

4. Drain in a colander and serve immediately with Bolognese Sauce and a sprinkle of grated cheese.

(If you wish to freeze pasta, allow to grow cold and put into suitable containers. Thaw before reheating in boiling water for 2 or 3 minutes. Strain and use immediately. Not as good as freshly made pasta but useful to have as a standby.)

BOLOGNESE SAUCE
4 generous helpings

Imperial (Metric)	American
1 medium-sized onion, peeled	1 medium-sized onion, peeled
1 tablespoonful sunflower oil	1 tablespoonful sunflower oil
1 clove garlic, peeled	1 clove garlic, peeled
4 small mushrooms, chopped	4 small mushrooms, chopped
4 oz (100g) lean, minced beef	1 cupful lean, ground beef
½ a small green pepper, de-seeded and chopped	½ a small green pepper, de-seeded and chopped
4 medium-sized tomatoes, sliced	4 medium-sized tomatoes, sliced
1 tablespoonful gluten-free soy sauce	1½ tablespoonsful gluten-free soy sauce
Sea salt and freshly ground black pepper	Sea salt and freshly ground black pepper

1. Chop the onion and fry in the oil until transparent.

2. Add the minced (ground) beef and fry lightly, turning it over with a spatula until cooked.

3. Put in the garlic (crushed), mushrooms, peppers and tomatoes.

4. Mix and season with the soy sauce and salt and pepper.

5. Heat through and cook for about 10 minutes while you stir.

6. Serve hot on special gluten-free pasta, sprinkled with grated cheese.

This can be re-heated the following day. Store overnight in the fridge, in a sealed container.

BAKED FISH

Imperial (Metric)	American
1 portion cod or haddock, filleted	1 portion cod or haddock, filleted
Sea salt and freshly ground black pepper to taste	Sea salt and freshly ground black pepper to taste
Juice of ½ a lemon	Juice of ½ a lemon
Rind of 1 orange	Rind of 1 orange
Small knob of butter	Small knob of butter

1. Preheat oven at 375°F/190°C (Gas Mark 5).

2. Put the fish in a shallow ovenproof dish and season.

3. Pour the juice over the fish and sprinkle with the rind.

4. Dot with butter and bake uncovered for about 15 minutes near the top of the oven.

5. Serve immediately with stir-fry vegetable or savoury rice (page 74-5). Garnish with a sprinkling of parsley and a slice of lemon.

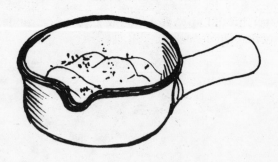

9.

PUDDINGS

FRUIT ON BREAD

Imperial (Metric)
1 portion stewed, sweetened fruit
   such as plums
2 slices special gluten-free bread
Vegetable oil for frying
Raw cane sugar for sprinkling

American
1 portion stewed, sweetened fruit
   such as plums
2 slices special gluten-free bread
Vegetable oil for frying
Raw cane sugar for sprinkling

1. Heat the fruit and keep warm.

2. Fry the bread in shallow, hot oil on one side only. Put on to a
    warmed plate and top with the fruit.

3. Sprinkle with sugar and serve.

Variation: Any fruit from the plum family will do — damsons,
greengages etc. (This is a very simple dish but really delicious. Other
fruits such as apple are not half as good.)

PEARS IN WINE

Imperial (Metric)	American
1 stewing pear	1 stewing pear
1 glassful red wine	1 glassful red wine
4 good pinches of cinnamon	4 good pinches of cinnamon
Raw cane sugar to taste	Raw cane sugar to taste

1. Peel and quarter the pear and place it in a small saucepan.

2. Pour the wine over the pear and cook over a gentle heat until the pear is soft.

3. Sprinkle in the cinnamon and sugar to taste.

4. Serve warm or cold.

Note: If the liquid reduces too much while the pear is cooking, then top up with water. (This can also be cooked in the oven in a small casserole.)

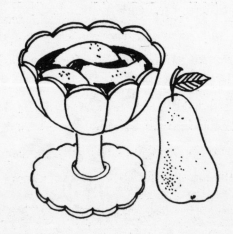

CRUNCHY DATE TART
Pastry:

Imperial (Metric)	American
2 oz (50g) polyunsaturated soft margarine	¼ cupful polyunsaturated soft margarine
4 oz (100g) ground brown rice	½ cupful ground brown rice
3 oz (75g) finely grated apple	1 small apple, finely grated

Filling:

Imperial (Metric)	American
4 oz (100g) chopped cooking dates (or stoned eating dates)	⅔ cupful chopped cooking dates (or stoned eating dates)
Approx. ⅓ pint (200ml) water	Approx. ¾ cupful water
1½ oz (40g) chopped nuts	Approx. ¾ cupful chopped nuts
Sprinkling of sesame seeds	Sprinkling of sesame seeds

1. Preheat oven at 425°F/220°C (Gas Mark 7).

2. Put the dates into a small saucepan with the water and cook until they form a stiff paste. Leave to cool.

3. Use a fork to blend the pastry ingredients. Knead into one ball of dough.

4. Grease a pie plate and line it with the dough by pressing out evenly with the fingers.

5. Raise a slight edge all the way round.

6. Spread the date mixture over the pastry.

6. Sprinkle with the nuts and seeds, pressing them in slightly.

8. Bake on the top shelf for about 20-25 minutes.

ORANGE CARAMEL

Imperial (Metric)	American
1 large orange	1 large orange
1 heaped teaspoonful raw cane sugar	1 heaped teaspoonful raw cane sugar
1 tablespoonful water	1 tablespoonful water

1. Pare off half the orange rind as thinly as you can and cut into strips.

2. Cut off the remaining rind and the white, bitter pith.

3. Slice the orange and place it in a serving dish.

4. Put the strips of rind into a small saucepan and sprinkle with the sugar. Add the water.

5. Heat while you stir until the sugar has melted.

6. Continue heating and stirring until you have a bubbly golden brown caramel. Pour this quickly over the orange.

7. Allow to cool, then chill in the fridge. Serve cold.

APRICOT TART WITH ALMONDS

A refreshing pudding that can be served all year round, hot or cold.

Pastry:

Imperial (Metric)	American
2 oz (50g) polyunsaturated soft margarine	¼ cupful polyunsaturated soft margarine
4 oz (100g) ground brown rice	½ cupful ground brown rice
3 oz (75g) grated apple	1 small apple, grated

Filling:

Imperial (Metric)	American
6 oz (150g) dried apricots	1 cupful dried apricots
2 heaped teaspoonsful raw cane sugar	2 heaped teaspoonsful raw cane sugar
½ pint (¼ litre) cold water	1⅓ cupsful cold water
2 teaspoonsful fresh lemon juice	2 teaspoonsful fresh lemon juice
1 oz (25g) chopped, shelled almonds	¼ cupful chopped, salted almonds

1. Preheat oven at 425°F/220°C (Gas Mark 7).

2. Pick over and wash the apricots before chopping them into small pieces.

3. Put into a saucepan with the sugar water and lemon juice. Bring to the boil and simmer until all the water has been absorbed.

4. Use a fork to blend the margarine, ground rice and apple. Knead until one ball of dough is formed.

5. Grease an enamel pie plate and put the dough in the centre. Flatten with the palm and fingers until it has spread evenly over the plate. Raise a slight edge all the way round with the fingers.

6. Spread the filling evenly over the pastry and sprinkle with the almonds.

7. Bake for 20 to 25 minutes on the top shelf and serve hot or cold in slices.

FRUIT TART

Imperial (Metric)	American
2 oz (50g) polyunsaturated soft margarine	¼ cupful polyunsaturated soft margarine
4 oz (100g) ground brown rice	½ cupful ground brown rice
3 oz (finely grated apple	1 small apple, finely grated
4 portions stewing fruit	4 portions stewing fruit
⅓ pint (200ml) or less of water	¾ cupful or less of water
Raw cane sugar to taste	Raw cane sugar to taste

1. Preheat oven at 425°F/220°C (Gas Mark 7).

2. Use a fork to blend the margarine, ground rice and grated apple. Knead in the bowl until it forms one ball of dough.

3. Grease an enamel pie plate and put the dough in the centre. Flatten with the palm of the hand and press out to cover the plate evenly. Raise an edge all the way round with the fingers.

4. Bake on the top shelf for about 20 minutes.

5. Prepare the fruit and stew it in a little water. Sweeten to taste.

6. When the base has baked take it out of the oven and spread with the stewed fruit. Serve hot or cold, cut in wedges.

Note: Blackberry and apple, plums, damsons etc. are particularly suitable for this recipe.

Variation: Make the pastry base but bake for only 15 minutes. Take out of the oven and cover with a thin layer of raw sugar apricot jam (jelly). Cover this with overlapping thin slices of apple. Sprinkle with raw cane sugar and put back in the oven for another 10 minutes. Serve as Apple Tart.

Make the pastry base and bake for the full time. Spread with raw sugar jam when it comes out of the oven. Serve warm or cold as Jam Tart.

Make the pastry base and bake for only 15 minutes. Take out of the oven and spread with black treacle (molasses). Sprinkle with special wheat-free breadcrumbs and put back in the oven for another 10 minutes. Serve hot or cold as Treacle Tart.

APPLE FRITTERS
(Serves 4)

Imperial (Metric)	American
2 oz (50g) potato flour (farina)	⅓ cupful potato flour (farina)
½ teaspoonful dried apple pectin	½ teaspoonful dried apple pectin
1 tablespoonful soya flour	1 tablespoonful soya flour
5 tablespoonsful cold water	6 tablespoonsful cold water
2 medium-sized cooking apples	2 medium-sized cooking apples
Sunflower oil, or similar, for frying	Sunflower oil, or similar, for frying
Raw cane sugar for sprinkling	Raw cane sugar for sprinkling

1. Put a serving plate to warm.

2. Mix the potato flour, pectin, soya flour and cold water in a bowl. Beat to a creamy batter.

2. Peel and core the apples and cut them into wedges — each one should make 8 wedges.

3. Dip these in the batter so that they are evenly coated all over.

4. Fry in shallow, hot oil, turning once, until brown. This will take about a minute each side.

5. Serve on warmed plates sprinkled with a little sugar.

Variation: Also use this batter for banana slices. (This recipe is delicious enough to serve to the whole family.)

CAROB PUDDING
(Serves 2)

Imperial (Metric)	American
½ pint (¼ litre) cold water	1⅓ cupsful cold water
2 slightly heaped tablespoonsful ground brown rice	2½ slightly heaped tablespoonsful ground brown rice
2 teaspoonsful vegetable oil	2 teaspoonsful vegetable oil
3 heaped teaspoonsful raw cane sugar	3 heaped teaspoonsful raw cane sugar
½ oz (15g) ground almonds	1 tablespoonful ground almonds
1 heaped teaspoonful carob powder	1 heaped teaspoonful carob powder

1. Put the water and ground rice into a saucepan. Mix until smooth.

2. Add the oil and sugar and heat to boiling point. Cook while stirring for about 3 or 4 minutes, or until the pudding thickens.

3. Mix in the ground almonds and carob powder.

4. Serve hot or cold in 2 individual glasses.

Variation: Sprinkle with flaked almonds before serving.

FRUIT AND NUT CRUMBLE
(Serves 2)

Imperial (Metric)	American
2 portions sweetened, stewed fruit — any kind in season	2 portions sweetened, stewed fruit — any kind in season
1 tablespoonful sunflower oil or similar	1 tablespoonful sunflower oil or similar
½ oz (15g) ground almonds	1 tablespoonful ground almonds
4 oz (100g) ground brown rice	½ cupful ground brown rice
3 teaspoonsful raw cane sugar	3 teaspoonsful raw cane sugar

1. Preheat oven at 425°F/220°C (Gas Mark 7).

2. Put the stewed fruit into a small ovenproof dish and flatten the top evenly.

3. Put all other ingredients into a mixing bowl and rub in with the fingers until the mixture resembles very fine breadcrumbs.

4. Spoon the crumble evenly over the stewed fruit, covering it all over. Make a hole in the centre to let out the steam.

5. Bake for about 10 to 12 minutes, until golden brown.

6. Serve hot or cold.

BAKED BANANAS
(Serves 4)

A simple but delicious pudding.

Imperial (Metric)	American
4 bananas, peeled and cut in half lengthways	4 bananas, peeled and cut in half lengthways
3 oz (75g) raw cane sugar	½ cupful raw cane sugar
Juice of 2 small oranges	Juice of 2 small oranges
1 oz (25g) polyunsaturated soft margarine	2½ tablespoonsful polyunsaturated soft margarine

1. Preheat oven at 350°F/180°C (Gas Mark 4).

2. Put the halved bananas in an ovenproof dish.

3. Sprinkle with the sugar and pour the orange juice over the fruit.

4. Dot with the margarine.

5. Bake for about 15 minutes on the top shelf.

6. Serve hot on warmed plates.

FRUMBLE

A quick pudding for one and a good way of using up special bread.

Imperial (Metric)

1 slice special gluten-free bread

½ oz (15g) polyunsaturated soft margarine

1 portion hot, sweetened stewed fruit

A little raw cane sugar

American

1 slice special gluten-free bread

1 tablespoonful polyunsaturated soft margarine

1 portion hot, sweetened stewed fruit

A little raw cane sugar

1. Crumble the bread by hand into coarse crumbs.

2. Melt the margarine in a frying pan (skillet) and add the crumbs.

3. Fry while turning them over with a spatula, until golden brown and crisp.

4. Spoon over the hot fruit, sprinkle with a little sugar and serve.

THREE-FRUIT SALAD

Imperial (Metric)	American
1 eating apple	1 eating apple
1 small orange	1 small orange
1 banana	1 banana
1 small glassful unsweetened fruit juice (orange or pineapple)	1 small glassful unsweetened fruit juice (orange or pineapple)
Raw cane sugar	Raw cane sugar

1. Prepare the fruits and cut into slices.

2. Pour the juice over the fruit and sprinkle with sugar to taste.

Variation: Other fruits in season can be used, e.g. pineapple, peach, strawberries, raspberries, nectarines, tangerines etc. Do not use more than three types of fruit. Clear honey can be used instead of sugar. (This is the easiest of puddings and can be eaten all the year round. Leave the skin on the apple for extra fibre and colour.)

RASPBERRY CREAM
(Serves 3)

Imperial (Metric)	American
½ lb (¼ kilo) raspberries	2 cupsful raspberries
5 tablespoonsful water	6 tablespoonsful water
2 oz (50g) raw cane sugar	⅓ cupful raw cane sugar
¼ oz (7g) gelatine, dissolved in 2 tablespoonsful cold water	1 teaspoonful gelatin, dissolved in 2½ tablespoonsful cold water
¼ pint (150ml) lightly whipped double cream	⅔ cupful lightly whipped heavy cream

1. Pick over the raspberries and wash them.

2. Put the fruit into the blender with the water and sugar and blend to a *purée* (sauce).

3. Put through a sieve to remove pips.

4. Gently heat the soaked gelatine until completely dissolved, then stir it into the *purée* (sauce).

5. Leave until it is just beginning to set, then fold in the cream.

6. Turn the mixture into individual glass dishes to set and serve chilled.

APRICOT ICE CREAM
(Serves 3)

Imperial (Metric)	American
6 oz (150g) dried apricots	1 cupful dried apricots
1 tablespoonful fresh lemon juice	1 tablespoonful fresh lemon juice
2 egg whites	2 egg whites
3 oz (75g) raw cane sugar	½ cupful raw cane sugar
¼ pint (150ml) whipped double cream	⅔ cupful whipped heavy cream

1. Soak the apricots in water for about 2 hours.

2. Put the fruit into a small saucepan with enough water to cover and simmer gently for 20 minutes with the lid on.

3. Drain, saving the liquid so that you have 5 tablespoonsful (6 tablespoonsful).

4. After cooling, put the cooked apricots, the reserved liquid and lemon juice into the blender. Blend and cool completely.

5. Whisk the egg whites until stiff.

6. Gradually sprinkle in the sugar and whisk again.

7. Fold in the cream and apricot *purée* (sauce).

8. Turn the mixture into a freezer container. Cover, seal and freeze until the ice cream is solid.

9. Store in the freezer until required, and serve after transferring to the fridge for half an hour.

Note: This is a useful recipe as it can be made all the year round.

BAKED APPLE

Imperial (Metric)	American
1 large cooking apple	1 large cooking apple
Water	Water
Squeeze of fresh lemon juice	Squeeze of fresh lemon juice
Raw cane sugar to taste	Raw cane sugar to taste

1. Preheat oven at 350°F/180°C (Gas Mark 4).

2. Wash the apple and, leaving it whole, cut a line around the middle. This will allow the flesh to expand during baking.

3. Cut out the core with an apple corer and discard.

4. Put the apple into an ovenproof dish and pour in about ¼ pint (150ml)/⅔ cupful of water.

5. Squeeze the lemon juice over the apple and sprinkle with sugar.

6. Bake for about 30 minutes on the top shelf.

7. Serve hot or cold.

BLACKCURRANT DESSERT

Imperial (Metric)
1 slightly heaped tablespoonful
  ground brown rice
¼ pint (150ml) stewed
  blackcurrants
Raw cane sugar to taste
1 teaspoonful vegetable oil

American
1 slightly heaped tablespoonful
  ground brown rice
⅔ cupful stewed blackcurrants
Raw cane sugar to taste
1 teaspoonful vegetable oil

1. Put all ingredients into a small saucepan and mix until smooth.

2. Heat to boiling point and cook, while stirring, for 2 minutes or until thick.

3. Leave to grow cold. Serve chilled from the fridge.

APPLE CHARLOTTE
(Serves 3-4)

Imperial (Metric)
1 lb (½ kilo) cooking apples, peeled,
  cored and sliced
1 tablespoonful water
Polyunsaturated soft margarine
10 fairly thin sliced special gluten-
  free bread (see recipes)
Raw cane sugar

American
1 pound cooking apples, peeled,
  cored and sliced
1 tablespoonful water
Polyunsaturated soft margarine
10 fairly thin slices special gluten-
  free bread (see recipes)
Raw cane sugar

1. Preheat oven at 350°F/180°C (Gas Mark 4).

2. Stew the prepared apples in the water with sugar to taste.

3. Grease a small loaf tin with margarine.

4. Spread the bread with margarine and sprinkle with sugar. Line the tin with these, prepared sides next to the tin sides and bottom.

5. Spoon the drained, cooked apple into the centre and put on a 'lid' of 2 slices of prepared bread, sugary side uppermost.

6. Bake near the top of the oven for 30 minutes.

7. Serve hot, straight from the oven.

FRUIT BRULÉE
(Serves 1)

Imperial (Metric)	American
1 portion stewed fruit, sweetened to taste	1 portion stewed fruit, sweetened to taste
½ carton natural yogurt	½ carton natural yogurt
3 teaspoonsful raw cane sugar	3 teaspoonsful raw cane sugar

1. Put the stewed fruit into an individual-sized ovenproof dish.

2. Pour or spoon the yogurt over the fruit.

3. Sprinkle the sugar over the top of the yogurt.

4. Place under a hot grill until the sugar melts. Watch it carefully so as not to let it burn.

5. Serve right away.

REAL FRUIT JELLY

Imperial (Metric)	American
¾ pint (400ml) pure fruit juice	2 cupsful pure fruit juice
½ oz (15g) unflavoured gelatine crystals	1 tablespoonful unflavoured gelatine crystals
Muscovado sugar to taste	Muscovado sugar to taste

1. Put about one third of the fruit juice into a small saucepan and sprinkle in the gelatine crystals.

2. Stir well making sure there are no lumps.

3. Put over a very gentle heat and gradually bring to the boil, stirring all the time, to get out any lumps.

4. Add the rest of the fruit juice and stir well.

5. Put in sugar to taste and stir until dissolved.

6. Pour into 3 or 4 individual glasses and leave to get cold.

7. Transfer to the fridge.

8. Serve cold, from the fridge, with a little single cream if desired.

For the fruit juice use any single juice or a combination of juices. Orange, pineapple, grapefruit, liquidized strawberries, raspberries, cooked stoned prunes or dried apricots. Any left-over stewed fruit can also be used — blackberries, gooseberries, plums etc.

FRUIT, CHEESE AND SPECIAL BISCUITS

Many people will prefer to finish a meal with something that is not too sweet. Special gluten-free crispbreads or water biscuits (see recipes) and butter, a crisp apple and low-fat cheese will make a popular last course.

Strawberries, raspberries, pears and peaches in season can also be used.

10.

TEA TIME

SCONES

Imperial (Metric)	American
1½ oz (40g) maize flour	¼ cupful cornmeal
¾ oz (20g) soya flour	2 tablespoonsful soya flour
1½ oz (40g) potato flour (farina)	¼ cupful potato flour (farina)
Pinch of sea salt	Pinch of sea salt
1 heaped teaspoonful special gluten-free baking powder	1 heaped teaspoonful special gluten-free baking powder
1 teaspoonful dried pectin	1 teaspoonful dried pectin
1 oz (25g) polyunsaturated soft margarine	2½ tablespoonsful polyunsaturated soft margarine
3 tablespoonsful cold water	3½ tablespoonsful cold water

1. Preheat oven at 425°F/220°C (Gas Mark 7).

2. Put the first seven ingredients into a bowl and mix them well.

3. Rub in the margarine until the mixture looks like breadcrumbs.

4. Add the water, mix and knead to form one ball.

5. Divide into 8 portions. Roll into balls, then flatten them to make scones.

6. Place the scones on a baking sheet and bake near the top of the oven for 15 to 20 minutes until golden.

7. Cool on a wire rack. Serve split and buttered.

MADEIRA CAKE

Imperial (Metric)
1 oz (25g) soya flour
2 oz (50g) raw cane sugar
1½ teaspoonsful dried pectin
1½ oz (40g) potato flour (farina)
4 oz (100g) ground brown rice
¾ oz (20g) yellow split pea flour
1 oz (25g) ground almonds
1 slightly heaped teaspoonful special gluten-free baking powder
Juice of a fresh lemon and water to make ¼ pint (150ml)
3 oz (75g) finely grated apple
2 tablespoonsful vegetable oil
Grated rind of 1 lemon

American
¼ cupful soya flour
⅓ cupful raw cane sugar
1½ teaspoonsful dried pectin
¼ cupful potato flour (farina)
½ cupful ground brown rice
1½ tablespoonsful yellow split pea flour
¼ cupful ground almonds
1 slightly heaped teaspoonful special gluten-free baking powder
Juice of a fresh lemon and water to make ⅔ cupful
1 small apple, finely grated
2½ tablespoonsful vegetable oil
Grated rind of 1 lemon

1. Preheat oven at 400°F/200°C (Gas Mark 6).

2. Put all ingredients into a bowl and mix with a wooden spoon until you have a creamy cake mix.

3. Spoon into a medium-sized loaf tin, oiled and floured with ground brown rice.

4. Flatten the top with a knife and bake on the top shelf for about 40 minutes. (Test with a knife to see if it is done.)

5. Turn out on to a wire rack to cool.

6. When cold, store in a sealed plastic bag. Cut with a bread knife and use as required.

Note: The tin size is important. It should be approximately 7¼ × 3½ × 2¼ in. (185 × 90 × 50mm).

ALMOND FRUIT PASTRIES

Imperial (Metric)	American
2 oz (50g) polyunsaturated soft margarine	¼ cupful polyunsaturated soft margarine
4 oz (100g) ground brown rice	½ cupful ground brown rice
1 large eating apple	1 large eating apple
2 oz (50g) raw cane sugar	⅓ cupful raw cane sugar
1 oz (25g) ground almonds	¼ cupful ground almonds
Few drops of pure almond essence	Few drops of pure almond essence
Sliced almonds for decoration	Sliced almonds for decoration

1. Preheat oven at 425°F/220°C (Gas Mark 7).

2. Blend margarine and ground rice using a fork.

3. Work in half the apple, grated, the sugar, ground almonds and flavouring. Knead until one ball of dough is formed.

4. Grease a baking sheet with margarine and put the dough in the middle. Flatten the dough out to a round shape by hand.

5. Cut the other half of the apple into thin slices and arrange these in the shape of a wheel, overlapping them slightly in the centre.

6. Sprinkle with a little more sugar and the sliced almonds.

7. Bake for 20 to 25 minutes until the pastry is cooked and the almonds toasted.

8. Allow to cool for a few minutes then serve, cut into wedges.

BASIC SPONGE MIX
(Enough for 6 buns)

Imperial (Metric)
½ oz (15g) soya flour
1 oz (25g) raw cane sugar
½ level teaspoonful dried pectin
¾ oz (20g) potato flour (farina)
2 oz (50g) ground brown rice
½ oz (15g) yellow split pea flour
½ oz (15g) ground almonds
1 slightly heaped tablespoonful
   special gluten-free baking powder
5 tablespoonsful orange juice
2 tablespoonsful sunflower oil or
   similar

American
1½ tablespoonsful soya flour
2½ tablespoonsful raw cane sugar
1½ tablespoonsful potato flour
   (farina)
¼ cupful ground brown rice
1 tablespoonful yellow split pea flour
1 tablespoonful ground almonds
1 slightly heaped tablespoonful
   special gluten-free baking powder
6 tablespoonsful sunflower oil or
   similar

1. Preheat oven at 400°F/200°C (Gas Mark 6).

2. Put all ingredients into a bowl and mix with a wooden spoon until you have a creamy cake mix.

3. Put 6 cake (bun) papers into 6 patty tins, and spoon the cake mix into them.

4. Bake on the top shelf until golden — about 15 minutes.

5. Cool on a wire rack and eat on the day they are made. (Stale buns can be used in jelly, with fruit.)

Variation: For natural flavourings, add either the grated rind of 1 orange, or the grated rind of ½ a lemon.

Special baking powder: See back of book for details.

SPONGE BUNS

Imperial (Metric)	American
2 oz (50g) Muscovado sugar	1/3 cupful Muscovado sugar
2 oz (50g) soft margarine	1/4 cupful soft margarine
1 egg	1 egg
2½ oz (70g) *Trufree* No. 7 S.R. flour	1/4 cupful *Trufree* No. 7 S.R. flour

1. Preheat oven at 375°F/190°C (Gas Mark 5).

2. Line 6 patty tins with cake papers.

3. Put all ingredients into a bowl and beat to a cream.

4. Spoon into the cake papers and bake on the top shelf for 15 to 18 minutes.

5. Cool on a wire rack.

If you are unable to obtain *Trufree* flour, use the basic sponge mix on page 104.

GINGER CAKE

Use the recipe for Madeira Cake (page 102), but leave out the lemon juice and use all water instead. To the dry mix add 1 heaped teaspoonful of ground ginger. Make and bake as for Madeira Cake.

FRUIT SLICES

Imperial (Metric)	American
Left-over gluten-free pastry (from fruit tart etc.)	Left-over gluten-free pastry (from fruit tart etc.)
Dried fruit	Dried fruit
Milk	Milk
Raw cane sugar	Raw cane sugar

1. Preheat oven at 425°F/220°C (Gas Mark 7).

2. Roll out the pastry and cut into 2 equal shapes.

3. Sprinkle one piece generously with dried fruit after brushing with milk.

4. Cover with the remaining piece of pastry and press the edges together.

5. Brush the top with milk and sprinkle with sugar.

6. Cut into fingers and place on baking sheet to bake for about 15 minutes. Serve freshly baked.

CURRANT CAKE

Imperial (Metric)	American
2 oz (50g) raw cane sugar	⅓ cupful raw cane sugar
2 oz (50g) polyunsaturated soft margarine	¼ cupful polyunsaturated soft margarine
2 eggs	2 eggs
4 oz (100g) *Trufree* No. 7 S.R. flour	½ cupful *Trufree* No. 7 S.R. flour
4 oz (100g) currants	⅔ cupful currants

1. Preheat oven at 375°F/190°C (Gas Mark 5).

2. Grease and flour (with gluten-free flour) a small 1 lb (½ kilo) loaf tin.

3. Put all ingredients into a bowl, except the currants and beat to a soft dropping consistency. Add a little milk if the mixture is too stiff.

4. Stir in the prepared fruit and put into the prepared tin.

5. Sprinkle the top with a little extra sugar (optional).

6. Bake for 30 minutes on the top shelf, then lower the heat slightly for another 30 minutes.

7. Leave to cool in the tin for a few minutes then turn out to cool completely on a wire rack.

JAM TARTS

Imperial (Metric)	American
2 oz (50g) ground brown rice	¼ cupful ground brown rice
½ oz (15g) soya flour	1½ tablespoonsful soya flour
2 oz (50g) potato flour (farina)	⅓ cupful potato flour (farina)
Pinch of sea salt	Pinch of sea salt
1 teaspoonful dried pectin	1 teaspoonful dried pectin
1 teaspoonful special baking powder (see page 126)	1 teaspoonful special baking powder (see page 126)
1 oz (25g) polyunsaturated soft margarine	2½ tablespoonsful polyunsaturated soft margarine
2½ tablespoonsful water	3 tablespoonsful water
Raw sugar jam	Raw sugar jelly

1. Preheat oven at 425°F/220°C (Gas Mark 7).

2. Put the first 6 ingredients into a basin. Mix well.

3. Rub in the margarine until the mixture resembles fine breadcrumbs.

4. Add the water. Mix, then knead into one ball of dough.

5. Roll out the dough, using ground rice. If any holes appear, mend with a piece of the dough.

6. Cut into rounds with a pastry cutter.

7. Lift with a spatula and line patty tins.

8. Bake for about 15 minutes.

9. Cool on a wire rack and fill with jam (jelly) when cold. (Eat on the day of baking.)

FRUIT SCONES
(Makes 8)

Imperial (Metric)
4 oz (100g) *Trufree* No. 4 or 5 flour
Pinch of sea salt
1 teaspoonful bicarbonate of soda
1 teaspoonful cream of tartar
1 oz (25g) polyunsaturated soft
  margarine
1 oz (25g) raw cane sugar
1 oz (25g) dried mixed fruit or just
  raisins or sultanas
3 tablespoonsful cold water

American
1 cupful *Trufree* No. 4 or 5 flour
Pinch of sea salt
1 teaspoonful baking soda
1 teaspoonful cream of tartar
2½ tablespoonsful polyunsaturated
  soft margarine
2½ tablespoonsful raw cane sugar
2½ tablespoonsful dried mixed fruit
  or just raisins and golden seedless
  raisins
3½ tablespoonsful cold water

1. Preheat oven at 425°F/220°C (Gas Mark 7).

2. Put the flour, salt, bicarbonate of soda and cream of tartar into a bowl and mix thoroughly.

3. Add the margarine and rub it in with the fingers.

4. Stir in the sugar, dried fruit and water.

5. Mix, then knead to a soft dough using a little more of the flour if you need to.

6. Divide into 8 portions, roll into balls, flatten and then shape into scones.

7. Put onto a greased baking sheet and bake on the top shelf of the oven for 15 to 20 minutes.

8. Eat freshly baked, split and spread with butter.

Note: If you prefer, roll out the dough and cut into rounds with a cutter.

11

FESTIVAL FOOD

PINEAPPLE UPSIDE-DOWN CAKE

Topping:

Imperial (Metric)
2 oz (50g) raw cane sugar
4 pineapple rings in natural juice

American
⅓ cupful raw cane sugar
4 pineapple rings in natural juice

Base:

Imperial (Metric)
1 oz (25g) soya flour
2 oz (50g) raw cane sugar
1 teaspoonful dried pectin
1 oz (25g) potato flour (farina)
4 oz (100g) ground brown rice
1 oz (25g) yellow split pea flour
1 oz (25g) ground almonds
1 slightly heaped tablespoonful
   special baking powder (see page
   126)
⅓ pint (200ml) pure orange juice
1 tablespoonful sunflower oil or
   similar

American
¼ cupful soya flour
⅓ cupful raw cane sugar
1 teaspoonful dried pectin
2½ tablespoonsful potato flour
   (farina)
½ cupful ground brown rice
2½ tablespoonsful yellow split pea
   flour
¼ cupful ground almonds
1 slightly heaped tablespoonful
   special baking powder (see page
   126)
¾ cupful pure orange juice
1 tablespoonful sunflower oil or
   similar

1. Liberally grease a straight-sided, shallow, round ovenproof dish, about the size of a sponge tin. Sprinkle all over with the sugar and place the pineapple rings in it.

2. Preheat oven at 400°F/200°C (Gas Mark 6).

3. Put all the ingredients into a bowl and mix with a wooden spoon until you have a creamy cake mix.

4. Spread the mixture carefully over the fruit and fill in the gaps.

5. Flatten with a knife and bake on the top shelf for about 30 minutes.

6. Leave for 5 minutes to cool, then put a plate on top. Hold the two firmly together.

7. Turn the dish upside-down and lift it off carefully.

PARTY TRIFLE

Imperial (Metric)	American
1 sponge bun (page 105)	1 sponge bun (page 105)
Raw sugar red jam	Raw sugar red jelly
3 teaspoonsful sherry	3 teaspoonsful sherry
1 slice of pineapple or ½ a peach	1 slice of pineapple or ½ a peach
1 portion of gluten-free custard	1 portion of gluten-free custard
1 walnut and a sprinkling of blanched almonds to decorate	1 English walnut and a sprinkling of blanched almonds to decorate

1. Slice the bun in half and spread with the jam (jelly), then sandwich together and cut it into pieces. Put in the bottom of an individual glass dish as a base.

2. Spoon the sherry over the bun pieces.

3. Cut the fruit into pieces and place them on top of the bun pieces.

4. Make the custard and spoon it over the bun and fruit mixture.

5. Allow to cool and decorate with the walnut in the middle and a sprinkling of blanched almonds.

CHRISTMAS PUDDING

Imperial (Metric)

½ oz (15g) dried yeast granules
2 tablespoonsful lukewarm water
½ pint (¼ litre) orange juice
2 oz (50g) raw cane sugar
1 oz (25g) soya flour
5 oz (125g) ground brown rice
1 oz (25g) yellow split pea flour
½ teaspoonful each gluten-free
   mixed spice, cinnamon and
   nutmeg
2 oz (50g) polyunsaturated soft
   margarine
1 small eating apple
1 small carrot
11 oz (325g) dried mixed fruit
Grated rinds of 1 lemon and
   1 orange

American

1 tablespoonful dried yeast granules
2½ tablespoonsful lukewarm water
1⅓ cupsful orange juice
⅓ cupful raw cane sugar
¼ cupful soya flour
½ cupful plus 2½ tablespoonsful
   ground brown rice
2½ tablespoonsful yellow split pea
   flour
½ teaspoonful each gluten-free
   mixed spice, cinnamon and
   nutmeg
¼ cupful polyunsaturated soft
   margarine
1 small eating apple
1 small carrot
2 cupsful less 2½ tablespoonsful
   dried mixed fruit
Grated rinds of 1 lemon and
   1 orange

1. Put the yeast into a small basin with the lukewarm water and leave for 3 or 4 minutes to soften.

2. Stir to a cream and put the yeast into a large mixing bowl.

3. Heat the fruit juice until lukewarm, using a small saucepan.

4. Pour the juice over the dissolved yeast and mix well.

5. Add the sugar, soya flour, ground rice, yellow split pea flour and spices and mix again.

6. Put in the margarine and grate in the apple and carrot. Beat until blended smoothly.

7. Add the fruit and rinds and mix well.

8. Grease a medium-sized pudding basin (2½ pints/1¼ litres, 1½ US quarts) and spoon the mixture into this. Tie on a double greaseproof paper lid and make a string handle.

9. Lower the basin into a large saucepan about one-third full with boiling water.

10. Have either a grid or 3 metal spoons in the bottom to keep the base of the pudding off the bottom of the pan. Put the lid on and steam for at least 1½ hours. (Top up with *boiling* water if the level goes down.)

11. Put a warm serving plate on top of the pudding after removing the paper lid. Hold firmly together and turn the bowl upside-down. Shake the pudding out onto the plate and serve hot.

Note: This is a rich golden pudding that will give 8 helpings. Apart from its colour, there is very little difference between this one and the traditionally made type. Serve it confidently to the whole family.

CELEBRATION CAKE
(Rich Fruit Cake)

Imperial (Metric)	American
2 oz (50g) soya flour	½ cupful soya flour
3 oz (75g) raw cane sugar	½ cupful raw cane sugar
2 teaspoonsful dried pectin	2 teaspoonsful dried pectin
6 oz (150g) ground brown rice	¾ cupful ground brown rice
1 oz (25g) yellow split pea flour	2½ tablespoonsful yellow split pea flour
4 oz (100g) ground almonds	1 cupful ground almonds
1 slightly heaped tablespoonful special baking powder (see page 126)	1 slightly heaped tablespoonful special baking powder (see page 126)
2 heaped teaspoonsful gluten-free spice	2 heaped teaspoonsful mixed spice
1 heaped teaspoonful cinnamon	1 heaped teaspoonful cinnamon
3 tablespoonsful sunflower oil or similar	3½ tablespoonful sunflower oil or similar
⅔ pint (350ml) pure orange juice	1½ cupsful pure orange juice
6 oz (150g) finely grated eating apple	2 small eating apples, finely grated
2 oz (50g) finely grated carrot	1 small carrot, finely grated
Rind of 1 lemon and 1 orange, coarsely grated	Rind of 1 lemon and 1 orange, coarsely grated
1 lb (½ kilo) dried mixed fruit, washed well	2⅔ cupsful dried mixed fruit, washed well

1. Preheat oven at 400°F/200°C (Gas Mark 6).

2. Put the first 9 ingredients into a bowl and mix well.

3. Add the oil, orange juice, grated apple and carrot. Mix again.

4. Stir in the rinds and the fruit.

5. Oil and flour with ground brown rice an 8 in (20cm) diameter cake tin (round). Spoon in the cake mix and flatten the top with a knife.

6. Bake near the top of the oven for about 1 hour.

7. Leave for a minute or two before turning out on to a wire rack to cool.

8. Use within 7 to 8 days and store in an air-tight container.

Note: This makes a lovely, moist rich fruit cake. Nobody will be able to tell the difference between this cake and an ordinary one, so don't be afraid to hand it round!

WHOLEFOOD DUNDEE CAKE

Imperial (Metric)

¼ pint (150ml) pure orange or pineapple juice

2 heaped tablespoonsful raw cane sugar

¼ oz (7g) dried yeast granules

2½ tablespoonsful vegetable oil such as sunflower

3 oz (75g) eating apple, washed and cut into pieces

1½ oz (40g) fresh carrot, scrubbed and sliced

American

⅔ cupful pure orange or pineapple juice

2 heaped tablespoonsful raw cane sugar

½ tablespoonful dried yeast granules

3 tablespoonsful vegetable oil such as sunflower

1 small eating apple, washed and cut into pieces

1 small fresh carrot, scrubbed and sliced

Flour:

Imperial (Metric)

1 oz (25g) soya flour

4½ oz (115g) ground brown rice

½ oz (15g) split pea flour

1 heaped tablespoonful gluten-free mixed spice

2 oz (50g) ground almonds

American

¼ cupful soya flour

½ cupful plus 1 tablespoonful ground brown rice

1 tablespoonful split pea flour

1 heaped teaspoonful gluten-free mixed spice

½ cupful ground almonds

Fruit:

Imperial (Metric)

½ lb (¼ kilo) dried mixed fruit

2 oz (50g) chopped walnuts

Grated rind of 1 lemon and 1 orange

American

1⅓ cupsful dried mixed fruit

½ cupful chopped English walnuts

Grated rind of 1 lemon and 1 orange

Decoration:

Imperial (Metric)

1 oz (25g) split almonds

American

¼ cupful split almonds

1. Preheat oven at 350°F/180°C (Gas Mark 4).

2. In a small saucepan warm the fruit juice with the sugar. When it is a little more than lukewarm, pour into a liquidizer goblet. Sprinkle the dried yeast into this and leave to soften for a few minutes.

3. Combine the flour ingredients in a mixing bowl and add the yeast mixture and the oil. Mix well.

4. Add the apple and carrot pieces to the liquidizer. Blend and pour over the flour.

5. Stir well and then put in all the fruit, nuts and rinds. Mix again.

6. Oil a 6 or 7 in. (15 or 18cm) cake tin and spoon the cake mixture into it. Flatten the top and decorate neatly with the almonds.

7. Bake for about an hour on the top shelf.

8. Leave the cake in the tin to cool. Eat within a week of baking.

Note: This is a lovely, rich, moist cake that is hard to tell from the wheat variety.

APRICOT CHEESECAKE

Base:

Imperial (Metric)
4 oz (100g) any special biscuits
  made from a recipe in this book
1½ oz (40g) polyunsaturated soft
  margarine or butter

American
4 ounces any special biscuits made
  from a recipe in this book
3½ tablespoonsful polyunsaturated
  soft margarine or butter

1. Crush the biscuits into crumbs and put them into a basin.

2. Melt the margarine gently in a saucepan and pour it over the crumbs.

3. Mix well. Cut a piece of foil to fit the bottom of a sponge tin or a shallow, straight-sided dish.

4. Grease with margarine and spread the crumb mixture evenly over this.

Filling:

Imperial (Metric)
2 oz (50g) polyunsaturated soft
  margarine
2 oz (50g) yellow split pea flour
½ lb (¼ kilo) cooked dried apricots,
  liquidized in ¼ pint (150ml) water
1 tablespoonful lemon juice
Grated rind of 1 lemon
2 pinches of cinnamon
1 heaped tablespoonful raw cane
  sugar

American
¼ cupful polyunsaturated soft
  margarine
½ cupful yellow split pea flour
1½ cupsful cooked dried apricots,
  liquidized in ⅔ cupful water
1 tablespoonful lemon juice
Grated rind of 1 lemon
2 pinches of cinnamon
1 heaped tablespoonful raw cane
  sugar

1. Melt the margarine in a saucepan and add the split pea flour.

2. Fry for 2 to 3 minutes, stirring all the time.

3. Pour in the liquidized juice/water and all other ingredients. Stir well and cook for another 3 to 4 minutes until you have a stiff paste.

4. Cool a little and spread over the crumb base. Flatten with a knife and allow to cool.

Topping:

Cover with a generous layer of raw sugar jam/jelly (any variety).

Note: Store in the fridge and eat within two days of making.

SAVOURY STRAWS

Imperial (Metric)

1 oz (25g) cold, boiled mashed
  potato
½ oz (15g) polyunsaturated soft
  margarine
Pinch of sea salt
2 oz (50g) ground brown rice
1 heaped teaspoonful very finely
  chopped onion or shallot

American

1 tablespoonful boiled mashed potato
1 tablespoonful polyunsaturated soft
  margarine
Pinch of sea salt
¼ cupful ground brown rice
1 heaped teaspoonful very finely
  chopped onion or shallot

1. Preheat oven at 425°F/220°C (Gas Mark 7).

2. Beat the potato to a cream with the margarine.

3. Gradually add the salt and ground rice and combine with a fork.

4. Put in the onion and mix well into one ball of dough. (If it is too dry, add a little water.)

5. Press out by hand on a surface floured with ground rice.

6. Cut into fingers with a sharp knife and use a spatula to put them on a greased baking sheet.

7. Bake for about 8 to 10 minutes. (Do not overbake or they will be too crisp.)

12.

COPING GENERALLY

Packed Meals
Don't fall into the trap of putting up packed meals that are largely stodge. Try to imitate a meal eaten at home for balance. Soup can be taken in a thermos flask for instance. Salads can be packed in a screw-top jar with another small jar containing dressing to put on just before eating. Pack slices of cold meat between small sheets of greaseproof paper. Cheese can be grated and put into a small plastic container to be sprinkled over salad.

Instead of bread, slice cold cooked potatoes and put into a plastic box. Bananas, apples, pears and grapes make perfect snacks but don't forget dried apricots, raisins and sultanas (golden seedless raisins) as well as nuts of all kinds.

Try to make the basis of the packed meal a protein one — meat, fish, eggs, cheese or nuts. The energy part of the meal, bread and potatoes, should not be too much in evidence, nor should you pack too much sweet and sugary stuff. A slice of rich fruit cake is much better than chocolate bars or stodgy biscuits. If fruit becomes boring try fruit jelly which you can allow to set in a plastic container, or fresh fruit juice with an ice cube in a thermos flask for a cooling summer drink.

It isn't a bad idea to keep a note of just what you put into packed meals if you have to cope with this every day. You can then avoid too much repetition.

The secret really is always to try to make the special dieter's food enviable and this applies just as much to food you are sending out from home as the food you put on the table.

General List of Gluten-free Items

Bacon
*Chopped peel and cherries
*Cut mixed peel
*Desiccated coconut
*Cornflakes
*Rice Krispies (UK)
Brown rice
Ground brown rice
*Ground white rice
*Flaked rice
Tapioca
All kinds of cheeses (plain) —
   not spreads
Cream
Fruit Juices (unsweetened)
*Squashes
*Chocolate (good makes)
Cider
Wine
Sherry
Brandy
Butter
Margarines
Oils

*Wine vinegar
Fish (fresh, uncoated)
Fruit (fresh)
Dried fruit
*Canned fruit
Meat (fresh)
Milk (fresh or dried)
Nuts (plain)
Pickled beetroot
Pickled onions
Red cabbage
*Syrup
Black treacle
Honey (pure)
*Jam (jelly)
*Lemon curd
*Marmalade
Sugar (raw cane)
*Other sugars
Vegetables (fresh)
Natural yogurts
Tea
Spices
Coffee (pure)

*Not recommended as part of a wholefood diet.

Balancing Your Diet

The average Western diet has many faults — far too much fat, sugar and salt; too little of fresh vegetables, fruit and fibre-rich foods; too many over-processed junk foods etc. Try to avoid these dietary pitfalls and balance your diet in this way to rectify matters:

15% fats, oils (including cheese), nuts and seeds
20% meat, fish and eggs
45% fresh vegetables and fruit
20% special gluten-free bakery items, including bread

The basic food in a gluten-free diet is not balanced in the same way as a diet where gluten-containing foods are staples. Here are the basic food values in a gluten-free diet:

PROTEIN — meat, fish, eggs, nuts, dairy produce
FAT — cheese, cooking oils, fish and meat, nuts and seeds
CARBOHYDRATE — rice, potatoes, bananas, special bread and bakery items, sugar
FIBRE — soya bran, rice bran, root vegetables, dried fruits
VITAMINS AND MINERALS — fresh vegetables and fruit

A wide variety of fresh foods should give you all the nourishment you need for a healthy diet. However, food supplements (vitamins and minerals) can be taken if they are felt to be necessary. These should also be gluten-free (specially formulated) like the rest of the diet. (See shopping list for brands.)

Coping at Home
Some people can take the situation of having a special dieter in the family seemingly in their stride. Others are not able to cope quite as well. The dieter eats the wrong things and never seems to be really well. Perhaps the secret is to be really organized about it and if possible to get the full co-operation of the dieter.

Make sure your special store cupboard is always stocked up. Teach the dieter to cook for him or herself if at all possible so that they will be able to cope with their own food in an emergency or just to give the usual cook a bit of a holiday.

If you can prepare things that the whole family can enjoy then so much the better — this saves preparing two kinds of food. Try to present the special food attractively and make it appetizing. Whatever you do, don't make the special dieter feel a burden. This can lead to emotional problems within the family unit.

Avoid a dull routine of cooking the same old recipes. There are several books available on gluten-free cooking now and this kind of exclusion diet isn't the dreary type it used to be, thank goodness. There are a variety of gluten-free diet foods available too. Try your local health store for these.

Don't forget, foods made from *wheat starch* are like to contain gluten even though labelled 'gluten-free'.

Holidays

If going on a self-catering holiday you can take with you a variety of recipes made up, as far as possible, for cooking and baking during the holiday. For instance, you can make up a few of the bread mixes and take the yeast with you to bake as you need them. (Add the oil and water just before baking.) A rich fruit cake is a good standby and will keep a week at least. Biscuits can be made too and kept in an air-tight tin. Crumble topping can be made up and kept in the refrigerator (if there is one) and used as required.

If the holiday is not self-catering then you will have to take some of the special foods you know you won't be able to obtain. Again, a rich fruit cake is a good standby, also biscuits.

If possible, notify the catering manager or equivalent of the place where you plan to stay that you have someone in your party who is on a special diet. This can avoid misunderstandings with the serving staff who can take offence at someone whom they think is just plain finnicky and a nuisance. Very often it comes as a pleasant surprise that staff will take no end of trouble to make sure the special diet is accommodated. However, do not take this for granted and have some standby items just in case. As a general rule, catering staff, however well qualified, have no knowledge of catering for a special diet.

One golden rule — never go on holiday without your diet food list; and remember, hundreds of thousands of people cope daily with a special diet so you are not alone. Don't think of it as a terrible problem, just get yourself organized and take it in your stride.

13.
SHOPPING

General Items
(Available at supermarkets or grocery stores)
Spices
Cooking oils
Dried yeast
Fruit juices
Wine or cider vinegar

Specialized Items
(Probably available at health stores, delicatessens or large chemists/
drugstores)
Soya flour
Potato flour (farina)
Rice bran
Maize flour (cornmeal)
Yellow split pea flour
Trufree flours (gluten-free)

Very Specialized Items
(The *Cantassium Co.* has a mail order service, including export, for
people on special diets)
Pectin (dried)
Special baking powder
Ground brown rice
Yellow split pea flour
Potato flour (farina)

Maize flour (cornmeal)
Trufree vitamins and minerals
Trufree flours and *Crispbran* etc.
Write for details to: Dept GFC
                               Cantassium Co.
                               225 Putney Bridge Road
                               London SW15 2PY

Some small independent bakers sell baked *Trufree* breads etc. They
are usually very helpful if you need regular supplies and some will
bake special items for customers. Some will supply hospitals in bulk
(UK).

Special Baking Powder
Commercial baking powders are designed to work with gluten, and
gluten containing grains are often used in their manufacture. In a
gluten-free diet special baking powder is required. If you prefer to
make your own here is a recipe:

Imperial (Metric)	American
¼ oz (7g) potassium bicarbonate	2 teaspoonsful potassium bicarbonate
4¼ oz (115g) potato flour (farina)	¾ cupful potato flour (farina)

Mix these two ingredients together and store in a screw-top jar. Use
as required. Try the chemists or drugstore for the first ingredient.

Pepper
A word of warning about the use of pepper. It is common practice
in commercial catering to add wheat flour to ground white pepper
to 'stretch' this expensive commodity. It is therefore a good practice
to use only freshly ground black pepper when you are eating out.

INDEX